Crafting

Wiccan

Traditions

About the Author

Raven Grimassi is a practicing Witch and an award-winning author of twelve books on Wicca and Witchcraft. Raven has been schooled and trained in both southern and northern European-based Witchcraft and Wicca Traditions including Brittic Wicca, the Pictish-Gaelic Tradition, and Italian Witchcraft. His experience in Witchcraft spans a period of more than thirty-five years. Raven is the co-founder and co-director of the College of the Crossroads, as well as a member of the illustrious Grey Council founded by Oberon Zell-Ravenheart.

Raven has worked on the construction of several traditions, including the Aridian and Arician systems. He is currently creating a system titled "Ash, Birch, and Willow," which is designed to be a teaching and training system for seekers of all levels of experience in Witchcraft and Wicca traditions. Raven considers it his life work to ensure the survival of ancient Witch lore and legend along with the ancestral teachings of the Old Religion. He is an expert on Italian Witchcraft, and is the leading authority on the works of Charles Leland in this field. Raven has appeared on both TV and radio programs throughout the nation, and is a popular lecturer at festivals and conventions across the country. He also conducts a variety of workshops on magic, ritual, and personal power.

Crafting

Wiccan

Traditions

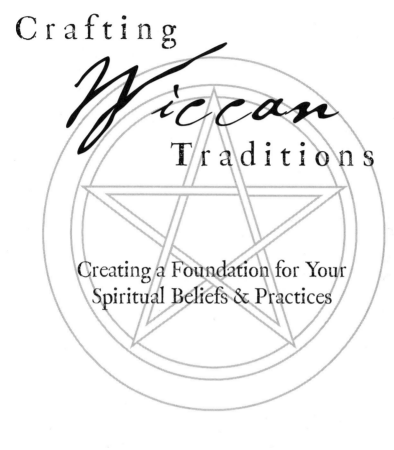

Creating a Foundation for Your Spiritual Beliefs & Practices

Raven Grimassi

Llewellyn Publications
Woodbury, Minnesota

First Edition
First Printing, 2008

Book design by Donna Burch
Cover art parchment © 2007 Dorling Kindersley / Getty Images
Cover design by Kevin R. Brown
Editing by Connie Hill
Interior illustrations by the Llewellyn Art Department
Llewellyn is a registered trademark of Llewellyn Worldwide, Ltd.

Library of Congress Cataloging-in-Publication Data

Grimassi, Raven, 1951—
  Crafting wiccan traditions : creating a foundation for your spiritual
beliefs & practices / Raven Grimassi. — 1st ed.
     p. cm.
  Includes bibliographical references and index.
  ISBN 978-0-7387-1108-9
  1. Witchcraft. I. Title.
BF1566.G735 2008
299'.94--dc22   2007047301

Llewellyn Publications
A Division of Llewellyn Worldwide, Ltd.
2143 Wooddale Drive, Dept. 978-0-7387-1108-9
Woodbury, Minnesota 55125-2989, U.S.A.
www.llewellyn.com

Printed in the United States of America

Other Books by Raven Grimassi

The Wiccan Mysteries: Ancient Origins & Teachings

Beltane: Springtime Rituals, Love & Celebration

Wiccan Magick: Inner Teachings of the Craft

The Witch's Familiar: Spiritual Partnerships for Successful Magic

Hereditary Witchcraft: Secrets of the Old Religion

Spirit of the Witch: Religion & Spirituality in Contemporary Witchcraft

The Witches' Craft: The Roots of Witchcraft & Magical Transformation

Italian Witchcraft: The Old Religion of Southern Europe

Witchcraft: A Mystery Tradition

Encyclopedia of Wicca & Witchcraft

The Hidden Path
with Stephanie Taylor and Mickie Mueller

The Well Worn Path
with Stephanie Taylor and Mickie Mueller

For Stephanie, who woke the sleeper and made life bright again

Contents

PREFACE

Defining Wicca in modern times is challenging, because the very nature of contemporary Wicca defies the type of structure typically required in order to present a definitive representation. In essence, Wicca is a religion that venerates Nature, and sees divinity reflected within all things. It is a path of personal growth and development that relies upon intuition and self-discernment.

Most modern practitioners view Wicca as a personal path that allows for individual interpretation and application of the beliefs and practices. The majority of Wiccans do not acknowledge any central authority figure, nor do they rely upon any set doctrines or "Holy Book" that is foundational and directive. Most Wiccans are self-directed and eclectic in nature.

The basic format of Wicca is built upon the beliefs and practices of pre-Christian European religion. Along with this is a blend of elements from Eastern mysticism and various forms of shamanism from different regions of the world. One popular inclusion is the system of chakras (personal energy zones in the body) and the aura, which is an energy field that surrounds the physical body. The basics that comprise Wicca today are both ancient and modern. In a real sense, contemporary Wicca blends ancestral knowledge and wisdom with the practitioner's needs in modern life.

The contemporary view of Wicca is very different from its presentation in the mid-twentieth century, which marked its public appearance. Wicca was once interchangeable with Witchcraft during the 1960s and through into the early 1980s. Today, most people separate the two, and view Wicca as a different system or religion. The most common modern definition is that Wicca is a religion and Witchcraft is a practice.

The word "Wicca" first came to public attention through the writings of Gerald Gardner in the 1950s. Gardner wrote about what he called an ancient fertility cult, which he claimed had survived into modern times. Wicca, as Gardner depicted it, was reportedly a fragmented system of Witchcraft, which focused upon a goddess and god of Nature (as well as being associated with lunar and solar veneration).

If you look up the word "Witch" in most dictionaries you will find that its root word comes from the Old English word *wicce* or wicca. The precise meaning of these words is highly debated, and some people argue that they refer to being wise, or to having the ability to bend and shape. According to historian Jeffrey Russell, the verb "wiccian" means "to cast a spell," and in such a case would link wicca/wicce to the use of magic. Russell notes that the earliest mention of the word "Wicca" is found in a ninth-century secular trial of a man accused of performing magic. Ironically many modern Wiccans do not practice magic, nor do some feel that it is even a part of Wicca today.

In the days of Gerald Gardner, Wicca was called the Old Religion, and was also known as the Craft of the Wise. Gardner claimed that he was initiated into a surviving sect of Witches/Wiccans who represented a lineage to ancient times. Modern scholars reject this and argue that what he presented in his books was primarily a modern construction. Others feel that, at the very least, Gardner added modern elements to the material he originally possessed.

During his writing career, Gardner presented Wicca as containing seasonal celebrations based upon the ancient Celtic themes of festivals known as Samhain, Imbolc, Beltane, and Lughnasadh. At a later time, he incorporated the festivals of the Spring Equinox, Summer Solstice, Autumn Equinox, and the Winter Solstice. This provided modern Wicca with the eight seasonal festivals of the year that now comprise the Sabbats. Over time, the names of the Sabbats have evolved. In the 1960s and early 1970s, they were commonly known as:

Hallowmas (October 31)

Yule (Winter Solstice)

Candlemas (February 2)

Lady Day (Spring Equinox, March)

Roodmas (May 1)

St. John's Day (Summer Solstice, June)

Lammas (August 1)

Michaelmas (Autumn Equinox, September)

The 1980s saw the names become almost standardized as the non-Christianized and Celtic-oriented titles:

Samhain (November Eve)

Yule (Winter Solstice)

Imbolc (February Eve)

Ostara (Spring Equinox)

Beltane (May Eve)

Litha (Summer Solstice)

Lughnasadh (August Eve)

Mabon (Autumn Equinox)

During the 1960s and 1970s, Wicca possessed a definite structure that included a set of laws. These laws described the hierarchy of the positions known as the high priestess and high priest, as well as established codes of conduct for covens and practitioners. Some laws set forth the physical boundaries for covens, establishing a three-mile territory for each one. Other laws established ethics and protocol regarding the use of magic.

The 1980s saw Wicca pass through an intense period of transformation. Innovative authors such as Scott Cunningham pioneered a new vision for Wicca, which ultimately transformed it into something new and different from many of its former and foundational concepts. Writers like Cunningham and others removed the traditional structure of Wicca and presented it as a self-styled and self-directed system. This approach has been called the "do whatever feels right" practice of Wicca. The majority of authors during the 1980s (and later) followed suit. It was during this period that the bulk of rooted and foundational concepts that originally formed Wicca were no longer passed on in the published material available to the public. Authors simply stopped writing about them, and instead presented their own creative views of Wicca, as well as various new methods of ritual and magic. The generation born in the 1980s (and later) naturally inherited this newly transformed Wicca, which was constructed through the ideas of a few pioneers.

Only a few of the many facets of the former Wicca were retained in the transformed counterpart. These included the idea of a goddess and god, the roles of high priestess and high priest, a level of degrees, eight seasonal celebrations, the use of a ritual circle, four directions and associated elemental natures, and a code of ethics known as the Rede. Some of these aspects are also disappearing, or being reinterpreted, as Wicca continues to be transformed by a new generation.

The majority of people involved in Wicca today are solitary practitioners. They gain most of their information about Wicca from published books and through the Internet. The Internet features various websites that provide information, and on the Internet one can also find many forums and chatrooms where discussions can take place. Unfortunately, the Internet provides as much misinformation about Wicca as it does useful and accurate information. While published books are subject to reviews that allow readers some insights about the material, there are few reviews of Wiccan websites that offer analysis of their authenticity and accuracy.

In most of the larger cities in the United States, seekers can find classes on Wicca that are held in Witch shops, bookstores, and New Age centers. These can be valuable in providing information, and for meeting like-minded people. Classes taught in person provide a means of asking questions and obtaining immediate clarification, which books and website materials do not provide.

Wicca Today

Modern Wicca is comprised of a diversity of beliefs, perceptions, and practices. Therefore it is difficult to provide definitive descriptions of it as a system, religion, or philosophy. In this section we will explore the most common elements of Wicca that share the basic consensus of agreement. At the same time, we will acknowledge that other views exist and may not conform to what follows here.

The foundation of Wicca as a religion is rooted in the concept of divinity being comprised of feminine and masculine polarities. These polarities are personified as a Goddess and a God. Wicca possesses a mythology in which the Goddess and God are associated with celestial objects, and with seasonal periods on the earth. The Goddess is associated with the moon and stars, and with the Sabbats known as the crossquarters (those that fall between the equinox and solstice periods). The God is linked to the sun and some planetary forces, and with the Sabbats that mark the solstice and equinox events.

The ritual practices appearing within Wicca are associated with the phases of the moon, and with the seasonal tides on Nature (as previously listed). The moon phases are metaphors for the Goddess, who is often depicted as a triple-image deity that is collectively known as the Maiden, Mother, and Crone. Here she depicts the stages of life: youth, maturity, and old age. As a goddess linked with the seasons, she is viewed as the Great Mother or Great Goddess. All living things are born from her, and at death return to her womb for rebirth.

The God figure is associated with the sun and its role throughout the year. Here he represents the periods of growth and decline as reflected in Spring and Summer, Fall and Winter. As a mythical figure, the God is the seed-bearer who impregnates the Goddess of Nature. From their union the bounty of Nature is given birth.

The eight Sabbats, or festivals, are known as the Wheel of the Year. The wheel reflects the changing of the seasons as the cycles of life. The myths associated with the Goddess and God are linked to each Sabbat, and depict a mated consort pair. Their relationship is reflected in the periods of Nature known as the waxing and waning times. The waxing, or growth-oriented period, includes the Spring Equinox, Beltane, Summer Solstice, and Lughnasadh festivals. The waning period incorporates the Fall Equinox, Samhain, Winter Solstice, and Imbolc festivals.

In addition to seasonal rituals, modern Wicca also contains rites that are linked to the phases of the moon. These are called the Esbats. The most common rituals are those of the new moon and full moon periods, which are observed monthly. While the seasonal rites can be viewed as associated with the phenomena of the material world, the lunar rites are largely linked to mystical or religious themes.

The religious aspects of Wicca include a belief in an afterlife called the Summerland, which is a temporary realm where the soul awaits rebirth into a new life. That process is called reincarnation, which is the idea that the flesh body is a temporary vessel used by a soul during many lifetimes. The soul experiences a variety of life situations as male and female, poor and wealthy, handicapped and physically fit. Through these experiences a soul learns the fullness of compassion, and evolves into a higher order of spiritual being that can serve as a guide for those souls still experiencing their journey through mortal life.

As a spiritual path, Wicca maintains an ethical philosophy known as the Rede, which is an axiom stating: "As it harms none, do as you will." Most Wiccans interpret this to mean that as long as no one is harmed by his or her actions, a person should do whatever feels right at the time. Another tenet in Wicca is represented by the "Law of Return" or "Law of Three," which states that every action a person performs (positive or negative) returns to them in triple effect.

Wicca does not present itself as the *only way* of spiritual enlighten-ment or evolution. The core philosophy of Wicca is tolerance, rooted in the acceptance of other belief systems and religions as being valid from their own perspective. The philosophy of Wicca does not condemn al-ternative lifestyles, and is generally supportive of those that remain out-side of mainstream society.

Now that we have looked at some of the basic ideas associated with Wicca, we can further explore its foundations. Our goal is to build a personal tradition based on a firm foundation, while applying our own unique views and interpretations.

INTRODUCTION

This book presents what some people might regard as opposing goals. The primary goal is to demonstrate various methods of creating a Wiccan system from the ground floor up. The other goal is to preserve the pre-existing foundations of Wicca. You might think that this is a contradiction, but it is actually a consideration of blending old roots and new growth. This is the formula in Nature, and after all Wicca is a nature religion.

The book is partially designed to present various older and traditional models of Wicca as it was known prior to the 1980s. I chose this time period because it marks the beginning of the changes that took place in Wicca, which have turned it into a religion different in several key ways from the Wicca I first encountered in the summer of 1969. The book is also designed to suggest methods of creating a personal system that is better suited to the practical needs of modern practitioners. It is my hope that this book offers the best of both worlds.

In laying out the ideas for this book into chapters, I wanted to provide various models that reflect the time-proven components of Wicca, and to explain why they are important foundational elements. I hoped that, by showing their continued relevance, the resistance to tradition by the new generation might be tempered. In addition to setting out the traditional building blocks, I also included ideas on how to personalize and be creative when deciding how to fashion a new system.

For those who object to changes, please know that my intention is not to encourage a new generation to abandon time-proven ways. For those who object to pre-existing traditions, please know that the intention of this book is not to shackle you to outdated and irrelevant material. Instead what I want to accomplish is to show both sides that Wicca can adapt to a new environment and a new time period while retaining its integrity and the momentum of its continuing empowerment from the past.

In addressing the topic of creating traditions, the book is designed for all levels of readers. I felt this was important because of the diversity of modern Wiccan beliefs about Wicca itself. I realized that any statement regarding Wiccan beliefs, concepts, and practices would bring disagreement from one faction or another. I also knew that the theme of the phrase "It goes without saying" could not serve the needs of this book. In order to have a common ground for understanding, the basics needed to be stated. I regard the definition of basics in this book as an "agreement of consciousness" between the reader and me.

I selected older foundational views as the starting point, which establishes and defines the basics from which varying views arose over the course of time. To this I have added the newer views, and among these I present some of the various interpretations and opposing views. I did not want to burden the reader with ongoing apologetics and endless prefaces on each page that not every Wiccan believes this and that. Let's have this understanding serve without repeating it throughout the book. I am hopeful that knowing this ahead of time will save everyone frustration.

For the intermediate and advanced reader I have woven in the metaphysical aspects that arise and expand once the basics are understood. It is my hope that the readers who are beyond the basics will look at them in this book as context for the expanded material. In this way any misunderstandings of the material can be minimized once the reader understands where I am coming from in what I present.

In the structure of Wiccan concepts and theology, several key elements apply to different aspects of the religion and magical system. In different contexts, the same theme can and does enhance the understanding and application. Therefore, a few things are repeated from various chapters in small sections, although not verbatim. Please know there is a good reason for doing so, and it is important not to skip over anything because you feel it's already been discussed. You will find that this is particularly true of material related to the Goddess and God and their seasonal and religious aspects. There are more facets and levels to this than you may think at first.

As the chapters continue, you will find that the material becomes more in-depth and addresses the metaphysical aspects of Wiccan rites, beliefs, and practices. These are important to the spiritual understanding of Wicca as a whole. In writing at this level, I am assuming that the reader has at least a nodding acquaintance with this type of information. However, so as not to put any reader at a disadvantage, I have included a glossary that contains the concepts that are not as common as others in Wicca.

Several chapters of this book are devoted to ritual themes, concepts, techniques, and structure. This will provide you with a great deal of information and examples through which you can formulate your own effective tradition. The keys provided in this book are the same keys used by people in the past to construct the ancient traditions. These vital keys are now offered to you in the pages of this book.

one

THE ENCHANTED
WORLD VIEW

Before examining methods of creating your own tradition, it is help-ful to look at various foundational elements. This is useful in un-derstanding the inner mechanisms of a tradition and how it interacts and integrates. It is from this understanding that you can draw out the specific components of your tradition that will support the religious, spiritual, and magical aspects that bind together whatever you create.

In this chapter, we will review the enchanted world view that is at the core of various beliefs related to spirits, deities, magic, and mysti-cism. Essentially, the enchanted view relates to spirits and forces that are supernatural and operate in the material realm. When creating tradi-tions, it is important to have a sound understanding of this view as it relates to nonmaterial realms of existence.

At the most basic level, we find a belief in the activity of spirits that influences human life. However, this can also occur indirectly as in the belief that spirits exert influences over crops, animals, weather, and other things that are important to human life. A direct involvement includes a belief in spirits intentionally bringing luck or misfortune to humans. Direct influences also include haunting and visitations from the dead.

The idea of offerings arose from a perceived need to honor or appease spirits or gods. It was an ancient belief that the dead could bring misfortune if they were unhappy with individuals still among the living. Food and drink were often left to appease them, and this ancient practice resembles the old idea behind Halloween. This was seen as a time when the gateway between the worlds opened, which allowed access between the world of the living and the realm of the afterlife. The trick-or-treat costumes represented the dead returning, and the treats given them were peace offerings.

Among the foundational beliefs, we find the concept of Nature spirits. These are perceived as ancient entities that are involved in the inner mechanism of Nature. For example, one very old belief depicts the opening of flowers and the emergence of fruit and grain as the end result of the work of spirits. In this view everything is the result of the activity of one or more spirits. Included in the realm of Nature spirits is the presence of elemental spirits of earth, air, fire, and water. These elemental spirits are the animating and activating forces behind the spiritual counterparts of these four physical elements. In essence, they are the creative forces that manifest within the material dimension. In classic occultism, they are represented by the titles gnomes (earth), sylphs (air), salamanders (fire), and undines (water).

A number of higher-level spirits are to be found in occult teachings. These are often called spirit guides, spirit helpers, allies, or co-walkers. Traditionally, these are beings in the spirit world that once lived mortal lives. Over the course of time, they spiritually evolved beyond the need for material bodies, and were released from the wheel of rebirth. They now serve the needs of souls still existing in material bodies. In essence, this is a spiritual fellowship devoted to aiding lesser-evolved souls.

One unique belief in Wicca is that of a race of spiritual beings known as the Watchers or the Guardians. These beings are often associated with stars, and in some teachings the stars are the eyes of the watchers. In other teachings, the stars are the campfires of the watchers in the night sky. Among the oldest associations of the watchers with stars is the connection of individual stars to each of the four watchers.

Traditionally, the four stars are: Aldebaran, Regulus, Antares, and Fomalhaut. These respectively mark the Vernal Equinox, Summer Solstice, Autumn Equinox, and Winter Solstice. It is the traditional role of the watchers to guard ritual settings.

At the top of the hierarchy of entities, we find the concept of the Divine Source of All Things, where it is personified as a goddess and a god. In essence they are two halves of the whole. However, in some traditions, the view is one of myriad self-aware deities that are not manifestations or aspects of an ultimate source. Whatever view one holds, the teachings simply point to the idea of deities topping the list of known entities.

The Goddess and God

In mainstream Wicca, we find the belief in goddess and god figures that appear as mated consorts. The Goddess is most commonly associated with the moon and the earth. The God is typically linked to the sun and the sky. The Goddess and God both possess various aspects including an association with death and realms of the Otherworld and Underworld.

In Wicca, the Goddess commonly possesses three primary aspects that are personified as the maiden, mother, and crone. These represent the three major life stages of the feminine. The God also possesses various aspects, which include a Triformis association. Here the God can be seen as the Hooded One, the Horned One, and the Old One. These present, respectively, his connection to the plant kingdom, the animal kingdom, and the kingdom of human tribal life. In the latter, the God is often depicted as the divine king or Slain God figure. This is his connection to agriculture, and specifically to the harvest where the grain is cut down, and the seeds are saved for the next planting season.

The Goddess and God appear in the Wheel of the Year, which represents the eight seasonal rites known as the Sabbats. In this structure they journey together through the year as a mated pair that empowers the forces of Nature. Four of the Sabbats mark the days of the two equinox and solstice periods. The other four festivals traditionally fall on the eve of seasonal days that mark the astronomical midpoints between the equinox and solstice days. In this view the God can be seen as associated with the day, and the Goddess is viewed in association with the night.

Magical and Mystical Realms

Ancient myths and legends tell of secret and hidden realms. These can be divided into two categories: the Otherworld and the Underworld. The Otherworld is perceived as the realm of beings such as the Elven and Faery races. This realm is sometimes called the Eternal Lands or the Land of Eternal Youth. Such names as Avalon are given to this realm, which is intimately linked to apples. In fact, one of the names for the Otherworld is the Isle of Apples. In old lore, carrying an apple branch known as the silver bough granted safe passage to mortals traveling to and from the Otherworld.

The Underworld is viewed as the realm in which the dead dwell while they await rebirth. In some traditions this is an inner realm within the Otherworld, and in other traditions it is separate and exists on its own. In some traditions, the Summerland of Wiccan belief is located in the Otherworld, and in other traditions it is placed in the Underworld. Wherever one places the Summerland, it is believed to be the resting place for souls just crossing from material life (and where they await rebirth).

One feature of myths and legends connected to the Otherworld/Underworld is the inclusion of a hidden or lost cauldron. These cauldrons possess mystical powers that can restore life, bestow enlightenment, provide limitless provisions, or transform anything placed within them. A common feature of cauldron tales is the placement of a cauldron in darkness, which is often represented by a secret place in the Underworld or deep within a castle dungeon.

Other realms outside of the mortal world include the dwelling places of deities. These are the Heaven worlds, and in some cases, the Underworld as well. Two popular examples are Asgard in northern European lore and Olympus in southern European lore. Among the oldest of teachings we find references to three great realms: the Overworld, Middleworld, and Underworld. Often these are associated with a giant tree, and in particular an ash tree. This tree is sometimes called the World Tree. The branches represent the Heaven or Overworld. The roots symbolize the Underworld, and the realm of mortal kind is the Middleworld.

Magic

The belief in the reality of magic is key and central to foundational Wiccan beliefs. However, it should be noted that some changes have taken place in Wiccan beliefs over the past several decades, and therefore some Wiccans do not include magic in their personal beliefs and practices.

Essentially, the idea of magic is rooted in the belief that the material world can be influenced by nonmaterial forces. One such force is an energy popularly referred to as magic. It is an esoteric force that can be tapped, drawn, and directed through various means. In Wicca, a system of tools, rituals, and spells are used to work with magical forces.

The ideas of magic helped early humans develop an understanding of the influences of the unseen. To this category we may add such things as illness, malformations, misfortune, and calamity. Magic provided a means of dealing with unseen forces, which allowed humans a sense of control. The ability to exert some degree of control within the enchanted world created a class of healers, magicians, witches, shamans, and cunning folk.

In modern Wicca, magic is often viewed as metaphysical science. It is frequently defined as the ability to manifest desire in accordance with personal will power. This suggests a departure from the ancient view of magic as a nonmaterial substance. In modern times, magic is often viewed as something generated and controlled by the mind. However, an earlier Wiccan view was the belief in two types of magic: raised power and drawn power. The former came from within the practitioner; it was his or her personal and developed powers. The latter came from another realm outside the material world.

The Astral Realm

A common occult teaching is the existence of a realm where thoughts can literally be transformed into material forms. The idea is that a realm exists consisting of an etheric substance that can bind to the energy of thoughts. Such a bound energy becomes what is called a *thought-form*. Here a strong will, empowered with a vivid visualization, draws the astral substance to itself. The substance then forms around the envisioned desire and creates an image of it. You can picture this as melted wax forming a coating on an object that has been dipped into it. In this analogy the wax is the astral substance and the object is the thought.

Once a thought-form is created, then the process of manifestation begins. This is because the astral nature has become dense and is therefore no longer in harmony with the astral plane. The thought-form is then drawn to the material plane where density is natural to the dimension. The book you are holding was once a collection of my thoughts that I desired to see manifest in material form. The book is a solidified thought-form. This is the essential principle behind the astral realm. It should be noted, however, that daydream thoughts lack the cohesion and intensity required to effectively create thought-forms. They do not attain sufficient density, and this is why they remain dreamlike instead of becoming a material reality.

As you work to create your own tradition you will, in effect, be establishing thought-forms. With dedication you will be able to draw power into your system, and you will be able to create links to pre-existing sources of energy.

The Elemental Realm

Among occult teachings we find the inclusion of a realm containing the nonmaterial counterparts of the creative forces known as earth, air, fire, and water. These occult properties are the building blocks of everything within the material realm. They also influence the mind, body, and spirit of all living things. In this sense, the elemental natures also have a profound effect on the emotions.

In essence each element contributes a quality toward manifestation. Earth provides substance, air applies transmission, fire brings about transformation, and water gives movement or motion. Another set of correspondences presents earth as giving stability, air providing expansion, fire lending vitality, and water allowing for adaptation.

The elemental forces work in conjunction with the astral substance to transform thought-forms into material realities. As an active force, the elemental realm can be viewed as a river that flows to and from the material dimension. Thought-forms leave the material world through the current of this river and pass into the elemental realm. Here they are bathed in the elemental natures that best match the desired manifestation (as contained in the generated thought-form). Once the thought-form absorbs the elemental natures, it is then passed into the astral fabric. Here it draws a coating of astral material, which in turn establishes a cohesive representation of what is desired.

When a thought-form appears completed within the astral dimension, its vibration changes, which causes the thought-form to be moved off and away from the astral levels. It then slips back into the elemental realm, which in turn passes the thought-form into the material dimension. This is because the elemental realm has already contributed its qualities, and so the thought-form moves to a dimension in which it can manifest its impregnated imagery. This dimension is, of course, the material world.

The Material Realm

In mainstream Wicca the earth is considered to be a living, sentient being. It births, nurtures, and hosts all living things. The existence of the material realm allows nonmaterial beings (such as souls) to experience this dimension. Living a material existence is believed to educate the soul and to teach it greater compassion.

According to occult tradition, the material world provides the direct experience of distinct cycles and phases. These are observed and learned through the changing of seasons as well as the life passages of birth, maturity, old age, and death. Here Nature is said to be the great teacher, for she reflects the workings of divine consciousness within her. This concept can be likened to the idea that the nature of the artist resides within the artwork. If so, then Nature contains the imprint of divine hands. This is one of the reasons why Wicca is a Nature-based religion that celebrates the seasons and cycles of Nature.

From a metaphysical perspective, the material realm is the lowest in energy vibration. The vibration is so slow that certain forms of energy become cohesive and visible. In other words, they look and behave as material objects. If we consider the fact that material objects are comprised of atoms and molecules, which are energies versus matter, then the teaching takes on scientific credibility. Another aspect of this teaching is rooted in quantum theories, which are too complex for the scope of this text.

In the teaching of reincarnation, it is said that souls become attached to the Wheel of Rebirth, which causes them to return and dwell in physical bodies. As these souls evolve, they eventually increase their spiritual vibration to such a degree that they can no longer be bound to material existence. In other words, the vibration is too high to become cohesive and visible in the material dimension; the soul sheds the density of the contamination of material existence through attaining a vibration that is too etheric to maintain physical attachments. This is when it passes into the spiritual realms that are harmonious to the soul's higher and refined vibration.

Between the Worlds

Among the many beliefs of occult tradition, we also find the concept of a place between the worlds. This realm is like a corridor or anteroom that exists between the material realm and the spiritual realm. In this sense it exists in neither realm, but actually resides in between them.

In occult tradition, the in-between places are the most magical of all. In addition to being assigned its own realm, such things as doorways and crossroads are said to be in-between places. It is at such places that spirits can reside. Here they can be directly encountered.

In Wiccan tradition, magical or ritual circles are often established between the worlds so as to operate in a mystical realm. Such a placement does not allow the laws of mundane physics to constrain the magical and ritual designs of the participant's intentions. The classic reference to the in-between realm defines it as a *place without a place, in a time without a time.*

A common traditional Wiccan belief is that the ritual or magical circle, once cast between the worlds, is enveloped by an energy sphere. The circle floats in the center and is shielded on all sides, above, and below. The placement of the circle between the worlds allows the energy of the ritual or magical operation to pass directly into the elemental and astral realms (uncontaminated by the dense vibration of the material realm).

Sacred Space

The idea of a ritual setting being sacred space is not a new concept, but its application within Wiccan rites is most likely a modern interpretation. Sacred space is often referred to in a ritual setting where a circle is created for a community gathering and left open but unbroken during the event. In this light, sacred space is a blessing and a containment of energy that protects and unites all within its influence.

The basic concept of sacred space, in its modern rendering, appears to be rooted in changes that took place in Wicca during the mid-1970s and early 1980s. During these periods the idea of a less-structured ritual arose. Previously the ritual circle was deemed a protective barrier and sphere that contained the energy generated by the people within it. Such a ritual circle required that an opening be made in order to release energy or to allow a person to enter or exit the circle. A modern view arose in which people could enter or leave a circle at will without creating an opening. This evolved into a concept that did not include the traditional understanding of the cast circle as it appeared in the older Craft understanding.

The concept of sacred space still incorporates certain aspects of traditional circle casting. Among these we find the evocation of the four elements, the call to the quarter guardians, and the evocation of the God and Goddess. Most people who use the sacred space concept still formally release the circle after the reason for establishing it has been concluded.

Now that we have reviewed the basics of Wicca's enchanted world view, we can move to the next chapter and begin our examination into crafting Wiccan traditions.

two

BUILDING YOUR OWN TRADITION

In this chapter we will explore ways of creating your own tradition or system of Wicca. The information and material provided here can help you decide how you wish to construct your own tradition of Wicca. You may want to go with a more traditional approach or a blending of your own views. Perhaps you may decide to create something entirely unique, which matches your personal needs outside of a formal structure. In any case, this chapter will provide you with suggested guidelines and tips.

Before we continue our exploration, it may be helpful to first define what we mean by a tradition. Essentially, it is a system that is based upon foundational beliefs and practices. It is a collection of cohesive and connected concepts that allows for the construction of powerful ritual formations. These will be covered in a separate chapter. The thing to remember is that a tradition expresses the foundation of your beliefs and practices. It is your view of inner reality and a map of how things operate in your mini-universe.

One of the values of a tradition is that it preserves and transmits the time-proven practices and alignments of the people who created the system. A well-established tradition teaches stages of training that are designed to present various concepts in a practical and functional order. This allows members of the tradition to receive teachings and techniques in a series of logical and connective stages.

When a student is acclimated to the foundational concepts, presented in a logical and connective series, his or her consciousness is directed in essential and beneficial ways. Naturally, this improves the understanding and experience of the teachings, beliefs, and practices of the tradition. Therefore it is helpful to map out the key elements of a tradition.

There are several foundational elements to consider when creating your own tradition. Let's look at each one and consider the importance.

1. Concept of Deity

2. Myths and Legends

3. Ritual Purpose

4. Ritual Structure

5. Religious or Philosophical Views

6. Training Format (materials/sources)

7. Hierarchy or Degrees

8. Magical Practices

9. Coven or Social Structures

10. Laws or Codes of Conduct

Look over the list and consider the information about each aspect. You may find that you want to use all of them, or perhaps you may prefer to select or modify in accord with your own preferences and views. Once you have an idea of how each one works, and what it contributes to the formation of a tradition, it should be easier for you to make your own informed decisions. Each of these topics is covered in more depth in other chapters.

Concept of Deity

Here we will assume that you have a belief in the existence of the divine source, whatever your view of it may be. It is useful to consider what you believe and how you might picture this and reflect it within the rituals and beliefs of your tradition. The easiest approach is to depict the divine source as being comprised of a Great Goddess and a Great God, who personify the polarity contained within the source. In another chapter we will explore how to choose a pantheon of specific deities. But for now the goal is to first apply your core beliefs about the Divine, and consider how you will work this into a tradition.

You may feel that you want to express deity only in terms of the feminine. This theme is found in such systems as the Dianic tradition, which views divinity as a feminine consciousness with male and female polarities contained within the Goddess. The possibility also exists that you may not want to express gender in any personified form. If so, be aware that this will make it very difficult to compose myths and legends that tie into seasonal rites. You can explore this more in another chapter devoted to creating ritual.

Another factor to consider is how you see divinity reflected within creation. For example, some traditions personify divine consciousness as a moon goddess or a sun god. Other traditions take the view of an Earth Mother and Sky Father. You may wish to consider how you want to express and personify the indwelling consciousness of the divine.

An easy way to address the issue of expressing divinity within your tradition is to use titles instead of names. For example, you can use "Lady of Nature" instead of a specific name for your goddess concept. In the same way you can use "Lord of Light" in place of a name for your god image. The chapter on selecting a pantheon will be helpful in guiding you in your consideration of a deity structure or presentation.

Myths and Legends

In modern Wicca there are myths and legends associated with the seasons of the year. These myths are stories that help to reflect the operation of divine consciousness within any given season of the year. For example, in the spring when life appears renewed in the return of budding plants, we find the story of the Goddess returning from the Underworld or Otherworld realm to the mortal world. When life appears to be slipping away in the falling of leaves from the trees, we find the tale of the God who dies and enters the Realm of Shadow.

You may wish to incorporate the myths that exist already in Wicca, or you may want to create your own. If your tradition is going to embrace the eight seasonal Sabbats, then you will find it easiest to use myths that relate to the changing seasons. One effective way is to think of a mated goddess and god pair who share a relationship as they move through the year. Here the myths depict them meeting, courting, mating, and producing offspring. Death is also a theme, and typically this is depicted as a dying god instead of a goddess. The God as the seed-bearer dies and falls into the earth, but the Goddess as the divine womb of the earth never dies in traditional Wiccan myth.

If you desire a full and complete mythical structure, you can compile a creation myth as well as the myths that comprise the seasonal foundation. You might find it helpful to explore the myths and legends of various cultures in order to get a good sense of the common elements. The commonality will assist you in understanding what our ancestors felt was important to include in myth and legend. Once the overall theme is apparent, then you can easily create your own mythical system if you desire.

Ritual Purpose

When considering what rituals to create, it is helpful to contemplate the purpose or intent of a ritual. Do you want your rituals to be ceremonial, magical, mystical, or celebratory? What purpose or goal will be served while performing your rituals? These are some of the ideas to think about in terms of creating the rituals of your tradition.

You might also want to consider whether to incorporate transformational aspects within your rituals, which is something found in the old mystery traditions of ancient times. This can be as simple as a sacred meal that represents union with deity, or it can be as involved as fasting and using methods of trance inducement.

A simpler approach to ritual is the use of a basic rite that features veneration or celebration. This type of ritual is less structured and allows for greater spontaneity and intuition. Here you can offer grain and fruit to your deities, while you sing or chant. Perhaps you may even wish to perform a dance or play a musical instrument as an offering. In a loosely structured ritual, intuition is the key and spontaneity is the directing force.

Ritual Structure

When creating your own rituals, think in terms of having a beginning, middle, and end. To begin a ritual, it is beneficial to state the reason for performing the rite. For example, in a group ritual the rite can begin with words such as: "We gather here on this first day of spring to honor and venerate the forces of rebirth and renewal. Today we welcome the Goddess of Nature who returns to us now in this season."

Part of beginning any ritual in Wicca is the casting of the ritual circle or the creation of sacred space. This establishes the physical area where the ritual will be performed, and it also aligns the participants to the spiritual quarters that mark the boundaries. In Wiccan terminology this establishes what is known as "the world between the worlds." This is a realm that is neither fully in the physical realm nor the magical dimension.

The middle portion of a ritual can be seen as the evocation of deity and/or spirits. During this period of the ritual you can include a symbolic drama play, or involve the ritualists in methods of raising energy through such things as drumming, chanting, dance, and so on. It is typically at this stage that any act of magic or spell casting is performed.

The ending of a ritual should include releasing energy and spirits, as well as giving thanks for the presence of your deities. It is during this stage that the ritual circle is dissolved, or the sacred space is released from mundane containment. Offerings and libations can also be performed during the ending phase of your ritual.

A common aspect of modern ritual structure is the incorporation of the four directional quarters of north, east, south, and west. Each is given a nature or characteristic, which differs according to tradition. It is also customary to assign an elemental nature to each directional quarter. See the chapter on correspondences for more information.

Another common feature in many traditions is the inclusion of mystical guardians known as the watchers or guardians. These beings have been described as evolved spiritual beings, angels, karmic agents, faery or elven spirits, and stellar beings. Essentially their role is to guard the ritual circle area against the intrusion of unwanted spirits, and to protect the integrity of the sacred space surrounding a ritual circle area. Traditionally, each watcher is assigned to an elemental nature and/or directional quarter. Various names have been used for the watchers, such as Boreas (north), Eurus (east), Notus (south), and Zephyrus (west).

Religious or Philosophical Views

You will find it useful to consider the basic belief system for your tradition. Some things to consider are your concepts of deity, the sacredness of life, reincarnation, an afterlife, codes of ethics and behavior, and your view of community. These can be organized and written into a blank book, which many people call a Book of Shadows. This book is a traditional record of rituals, spells, recipes, and mystical experiences.

Over the course of time, your views may change on any given subject. Therefore, you may want your book of shadows to be a binder where pages can be added or removed. At a later stage when you feel ready, you can set the beliefs and practices of your tradition into a permanent book of shadows. Traditionally, students copy from their teacher's book during their training. If you desire to incorporate this into your tradition, it is helpful to think about how you want to organize your book. You can find some guidelines in the chapter on the book of shadows.

One effective approach in establishing the beliefs and practices of a tradition is to decide what kind of system you want. Will the tradition be founded upon pre-existing systems or will it be innovative, and if so, to what degree? Is the material comprising your tradition an eclectic gathering or will it be rooted in a particular cultural expression such as Celtic, Germanic, or Italian? These are important decisions to make, as they will influence everything within your tradition from ritual formats to deity forms.

Before deciding upon the beliefs or views for your tradition, it is advisable to research a variety of tenets and philosophies from various regions of the world (ancient and modern). Being well read and well informed will make things operate more smoothly as other people join your tradition. These people will naturally bring their own perspectives and backgrounds with them when they become members. Therefore, you will encounter fewer conflicts when the beliefs and practices of your tradition share a commonality with other core beliefs found in the religions and philosophies of the world.

I am not suggesting that you abandon any contrary views that you hold, but I merely point out that a blend will help others to more easily acclimate to your tradition. However, a tradition should at some levels contain its own unique elements, and naturally the views of its founders will be central to the tradition itself. What is unique about a tradition is what often attracts others, and what is comfortable tends to help people remain within the system. Uniqueness is attraction, and familiarity is comfort.

Training Format

One important element within a tradition is the training and experience it offers. There are several key areas to consider. These include a grouping of categories: deities, myths and legends, ritual structure, magical training, arts of the Craft, core tenets and practices, codes or rules, and levels of advancement. Your tradition can contain them all, or can be focused upon several specific ones.

When creating a training program, think in terms of what you want the members of the tradition to achieve in the long run. An easy way to break this down is to examine what areas of knowledge a teacher of your tradition should possess. Do you want a teacher to have a command of some form of divination, and if so, which methods? Should he or she have a practical knowledge of herbs, the preparation of potions, or the healing arts? Do you want your teachers to have magical and ritual knowledge and experience? If so, you will need a plan to teach such things at various stages of the person's training.

There are other areas of knowledge that you may want your teachers to be able to address. These include historical and anthropological information and data to lend support to any claims you might want to make about the roots, origins, and foundations of your tradition. Unfortunately, there will always be people who desire to discredit the work of others, and you will find it less frustrating to be sure of your facts as you organize your tradition.

One final tip is to provide opportunities for your clergy to attend workshops on management, relationship counseling, positive thinking, and other areas that promote and develop good and effective people skills. At the very least, your clergy should be encouraged to read self-help books in these areas. A time will come when members of your tradition will need to turn to someone for help and support. You will want the best of your people available at such times.

Hierarchy or Degrees

When formulating your tradition, you may want to consider the idea of levels or degrees for members. This also includes any roles or positions that people may hold or fulfill. Some examples are priestess/priest, high priestess/high priest, coven crone, coven maiden, summoner, and so on. These are traditional roles that you may or may not want to include. For further information, see the chapter on initiation.

An element worthy of serious consideration is whether you prefer a Socratic or democratic foundation and system. The Socratic approach consists of direction given by a leader figure, while the democratic approach is directed by consensus. There are pros and cons to each system, and you will want to think about this structure. Related to all of this will be a decision whether to have an established high priestess and high priest who preside at each ritual. Or, do you want to rotate who presides so that everyone has an opportunity?

Common to most traditions is a degree system, which typically consists of three degrees. The first degree is the entry level, the second degree is the phase of the priestess or priest, and the third degree denotes the role of high priestess or high priest. When considering a degree system you will want to think about whether or not to create initiation rituals for each degree. If so, you will find helpful guidelines for initiation rituals in other chapters (as well as information on dedication rituals and time frames).

Magical Practices

One of the decisions in creating a tradition is whether you will incorporate magic and spell work. If so, you will want to consider the type of magical system with which you want to work. Will you focus on simple folk magic, or draw upon ceremonial magical systems that appear in traditional grimiores? Perhaps a blend of the two might appeal to you more.

If you use magic in your tradition, there are some considerations that you will want to explore. Bear in mind that the core of the source of power for your magic is directly linked to your beliefs. Therefore it is advisable to examine what it is that you believe in. For example, do you believe in the inherent power of herbs and minerals? Do you believe in spirits of Nature and the Otherworld? What is your connection to the things that you believe can empower your magic? Once you decide where the power of your magic comes from, then you are in a better position from which to construct your magical system.

As previously noted, a traditional aspect of Wicca is the belief in creative forces called elements, which are considered to be the universal building blocks for manifestation. The energies of earth, air, fire, and water are the nonmaterial expressions of their material counterparts. In other words, the elements are the energies associated with earth, air, fire, and water, as we know them in everyday life. It can be said that the elements are also spiritual or emotional as reflected in our personality and character. In the same way that people are said to be like their zodiac sign, so too can an elemental nature be a part of our makeup.

Elemental natures are an important part of Wiccan philosophy. In the magical tradition of Wicca, we find four traditional ritual tools, each of which are linked to an individual elemental force. These tools are the pentacle, wand, athame, and chalice. There are two main group associations related to the elemental nature of any given tool. The first group is rooted in ancient Pagan concepts, and the second group is derived from ceremonial magical systems such as the Golden Dawn.

Group One:
Pentacle is linked to earth and the north quarter of ritual circle
Wand is linked to air and the east quarter of ritual circle
Athame is linked to fire and the south quarter of ritual circle
Chalice is linked to water and the west quarter of ritual circle

Group Two:
Pentacle is linked to earth and the north quarter of ritual circle
Athame is linked to air and the east quarter of ritual circle
Wand is linked to fire and the south quarter of ritual circle
Chalice is linked to water and the west quarter of ritual circle

When designing a ritual circle for magical purposes, there are a variety of systems to draw upon, or you may wish to create your own. The suggested reading list at the back of this book will provide some helpful signposts.

Coven or Social Structure

A tradition typically contains a social structure of some sort, such as a coven. Generally speaking, a *coven* is a group of people comprised of from three to thirteen members. Some people prefer to use the terms "fellowship" or "grove" instead of coven. When forming a group there are some basic things to consider, such as whether your coven will require a rite of initiation in order for a person to become a member. Another consideration is the oath of secrecy or privacy so that everyone feels safe in the intimate setting of a coven structure.

It is customary for a coven to perform ritual either dressed in robes or some other ritual attire, or to be "sky clad" (without anyone clothed). Whatever your preference may be, it is advisable for the coven to dress (or undress) specifically for ritual as this creates a sense of the special nature and bond of the group. You may want to name the group after something symbolic, such as a mythical creature, a constellation, or a sacred place. One example is Stonehenge Coven, and another is Coven of the North Star.

As previously mentioned, you will want to consider how the directing roles will function. Do you want to have fixed positions of high priestess and high priest from which these specific individuals facilitate ritual, or do you prefer rotating the coven members as facilitators?

Another element related to the coven is the process by which members are added. Traditionally, this is done by a unanimous vote, and any dissenting vote negates the proposed member. The reason for this approach is to ensure complete acceptance and harmony within the coven membership. Another aspect to consider is whether attendance at a ritual or celebration is mandatory or optional for coven members. All of these things influence mental and emotional health, and therefore are important considerations for the well-being of the coven.

Laws or Codes of Conduct

Consider whether your tradition will have formal laws or some system of guidelines. You may ultimately decide that it will not include anything of this nature, but it is wise to have an established plan. It has been my experience that providing expectations related to the behavior of the members within your tradition works best. This way everyone knows in advance what is expected from him or her.

It is wise to not only write out what the law states, but to also include what the law is intended to accomplish or prevent. This will help other people in the future to understand what these laws were all about, which will make it clear what the spirit of the law intended versus what the wording appears to indicate. In this way, there will be less argument over the need for the laws, and less misinterpretation when applying the law to whatever circumstances arise.

If you choose to have a system of laws, then consider what consequences apply when these laws are broken. Think about intent—will it matter why the law was broken, or is the letter of the law to prevail? Bear in mind that when a law is broken for even the best of intentions, the impact upon other people can still be a very negative experience. However, laws that are strictly enforced as written, without any personal consideration, can result in people leaving your tradition because it appears too harsh.

It has been my experience that a beneficial system outlines the expectations for attending rituals, and establishes social codes of conduct that are simple and do not intrude into the personal lives of the tradition's members. Will everyone be required to attend all of the yearly Sabbats? What about the monthly lunar rites? In my experience, the healthiest covens were those whose members were able to build strong personal bonds. These bonds came from being together as a family for all of the tradition's rituals. However, I have also discovered that some people are not happy in a system that requires them to do anything. You will want to give the matter some serious thought. In the end, I believe you will find that the needs of the many outweigh the needs of the one.

Now that we have looked at the framework for a tradition, it is time to turn our attention to the concept of deity. How you view deity, and how you wish to interact with it, will determine the integration of the divine connection to your tradition. Therefore, it will be beneficial to explore this aspect of creating your tradition. In the following chapter, we will explore the concept of deity within Wicca, and methods of establishing a system that will incorporate a working relationship with the Divine.

three

FINDING YOUR PANTHEON

The concept of deity in most traditions consists of a mated goddess and god. Many traditions also include a host of other deities, which is called the pantheon of the tradition. It is important to explore the myths and legends of any deities that you want to include in your pantheon. It is advisable to have deity pairings that are harmonious or are balanced polarities to one another. In this way, you can avoid internal conflicts that arise when creating corresponding rituals, myths, and legends.

Many people prefer to work with deities that are connected to their nationality, such as Celtic, Germanic, Hungarian, Greek, Italian, and so on. One of the advantages of this approach is that it connects the tradition to ancestral roots. Something seems to stir in the blood when we link to the ancestral current of knowledge and wisdom.

Some people are drawn to pantheons that have no direct link to their own nationality. This may be due to a past-life experience that was uncompleted, or it may be a call to experience new teachings. The concept of reincarnation includes the idea of experiencing many different lives, connections, and conditions that allow for the full and complete education of the soul. Therefore, you do not need to be concerned if you aren't drawn to the deities of your bloodline.

Reading the myths and legends of various cultures is a good way of exploring and getting acquainted with a variety of deities. In addition, stories are a useful means of conveying metaphors related to the nature of specific gods and goddesses. The ancient models depicted deities as being pleased by certain offerings and offended by others. Each goddess and god had likes and dislikes, emotions, pet peeves, and relatively predictable responses within any given matter.

One way to view such myths is like a blueprint of energy that maps out the inner mechanism of how a specific deity operates. This demonstrates the interplay once the divine consciousness is stimulated. In other words, myths provide a working model of the nature and character of a deity as viewed from a human perspective, which can be used when constructing rituals.

A very simple truth to consider is that getting to know a deity is like getting to know another person. When we meet someone at any given stage of his or her life, what we encounter is the culmination of things that made this person who and what they are today. But the person in front of us today is only a specific reflection of the entire being as a whole. The future may bring changes of any kind. Therefore, to really know the person, we must ask the questions that tell us where he or she is from, how the person grew up, what events shaped his or her life, what the person's aspirations are, etc. Getting to know a deity calls for the same exploration. Without this we can only know what we are currently looking at, which is only part of the totality.

Whenever you read an ancient myth or legend, you are essentially looking at how our predecessors related to various gods and goddesses. Some of the things featured in a myth or legend are warnings about what angers the goddess or god within the story. Such tales no doubt arose from a perceived cause-and-effect observation, and it can be helpful to take into account the assessment of our ancestors when we work with any deity.

If you desire to work within the customary structure of the Craft, then you will want to select deities that align with seasonal and celestial themes. It is helpful to examine these themes in connection with a goddess and god figure. Once you know and understand the customary themes, then you can select deities that fit the model.

Agricultural Theme

One of the early concepts in Wicca was the idea of an Earth Mother goddess and her son, both associated with agricultural themes. Here the Goddess is the deep rich soil, and her son is the seed-bearing plant that arises from the earth-womb. Together they assure the cycles of Nature.

When exploring which goddess to incorporate into your tradition, think in terms of a fertile deity and one that is not a chaste or virginal goddess. A goddess who is associated with grain, fertility, or harvest is a good choice. For a deeper level of connection, you may wish to consider incorporating a goddess associated with journeys or events linked to the Underworld. This relationship ties together the theme of the planted seed and the darkness within the earth where the seed awaits birth.

The seed is the metaphorical son of the Goddess. It is birthed from beneath the soil, rises up a stalk, and eventually progresses to bud, leaf, and flower. The last stage is the appearance of the seed. This seed will fall as the plant declines or dies, and the seed sinks into the earth. Here is the representation of the cycle of life, as well as the mythical theme associated with the God through myth and legend.

The classic mythological theme depicts the rise and fall of the Sun God, who is both the seed of light and the physical seed of plant renewal. Here we see the birth, rise, and death of the plant as a representation of the cycle of our own bodies. The cycles of the sun (seemingly rising from the earth and falling back into its depths) are reflective of the soul descending into a physical body in a series of lifetimes.

The Pagan theme of the dying and rising god is also found in Christian theology. The original theme was a personal alignment with the God in order for the soul to be carried through the passages of the God.

In this concept is found the belief that the soul is resurrected through its intimate connection to the God.

In the classical mythology of the Goddess, we find her as the Great Mother from whom the God is born into the mortal world. Unlike the God, the Goddess never dies. Instead she withdraws from the mortal realm in a conscious act designed to retrieve the God from the Underworld. This is a metaphor for the life force stirring beneath the soil, which awakens the buried seed. In the myth of the Goddess, she follows the dying God into the Underworld, magically rebirths him, and then returns to the mortal realm. These events are marked by the Sabbats known as Samhain, Yule, and Ostara.

Celestial Theme

In mainstream Wicca, we find the customary association of the Goddess with the moon and the stars. Through these associations she is often called the Queen of Heaven, and is a goddess linked to the phases of the moon and to certain stars and constellations. The celestial nature of the Goddess demonstrates her higher self as distinguished from the Goddess as she is associated with the earth.

Her lunar nature represents the Goddess as a transformer and shapeshifter. Through the parallels of the moon's phases we can view the Goddess as manifesting in various feminine natures. When the moon is new, we see the maiden image. The full moon represents the ripe mother, and the waning phase symbolizes the wise woman. The stars connect the Goddess to Otherworld themes, realms that exist in the depths of the Universe.

The God is commonly associated with the sun and the sky. Here he is viewed as physically above the Goddess in her earthly manifestation. This holds fertile symbolism as the impregnator of the Goddess, who is the soul of Nature. The setting of the sun can be seen as entering the Goddess in sexual union. The rising of the sun can be viewed as being birthed from the womb of the Goddess.

The association of the sky with the God represents his higher self, as distinguished from the God as he is associated with the physical sun. The sky connects the God to heaven worlds that are immediate in nature for the souls crossing over from mortal life. These are the human constructions that appear in various religions, and are temporary abodes (although most religions do not view them this way).

Otherworld Theme

In modern Wicca we find the theme of the Otherworld, which is a realm unlike the afterlife or Underworld that is commonly depicted in most religions. In the older myths and legends associated with the Otherworld, it is a place where both the living and the dead may enter. It is often intimately linked to magical kingdoms, elven or faery realms, and enchanted lands.

The Otherworld is connected to teaching opportunities, spirit guides, and ascended masters. If you desire an Otherworld component to your tradition, you may wish to use legendary figures associated with this theme. These can serve as co-walkers who may assist you in Otherworld contact and work. You can choose classic figures such as Merlin, or you can work with various forms like the Crone of the Cottage or Walker in the Woods figures (see glossary).

One popular way is to use the elven or faery connection and work with these forms as contacts to the Otherworld. Statues, figurines, or paintings of these figures can be used as a meditation portal. You may even want to name your contact as a means of interfacing.

Triformis Goddess Theme

The idea of a goddess depicted in three forms or aspects is central to mainstream Wiccan theology. In modern Wicca they are called the maiden, mother, and crone. Here we can see the ancient model of the Three Fates, who in ancient art are depicted as a young woman, a mature woman, and an elderly woman.

One theme that appears in the triformis nature is the idea of the ancient three worlds: Above, Middle, and Below. Here we can see the concept of a goddess of the heavens, the earth, and the Underworld. When considering the selection of a triformis deity, you will want to bear these connections in mind. This is because the three worlds have an association with the eight Sabbats, which contain the mythos of the God and Goddess. The more the aspects of your tradition connect and agree with one another, the more solid and productive your system will be.

As previously mentioned, in modern Wicca the Triformis Goddess is intimately connected to the phases of the moon. The cycles of the moon are reflected in the menstrual cycle of women, and here we find an intimate connection between the Goddess and women. This is one of the reasons why the triple nature of the Goddess is divided into maiden, mother, and crone. These are the cycles of womanhood that are marked by bleeding and its cessation (the presence and absence of fertility).

On a more universal level, the aspects of the Triformis Goddess relate to magical and mundane themes. The maiden aspect is seen as the innovator and the vitality of renewal. New beginnings and new ventures are associated with the maiden. The mother aspect is viewed as the birthing and nurturing, bringing things to their fullness. Protecting, caring, and sustaining are associated with the mother. The crone is seen as preserving and reflecting upon the inner nature, for she is wisdom gained from experience.

Triformis God Theme

In modern Wicca we can divide the God into three aspects that compliment the Triformis Goddess. These aspects are called: the horned one, the hooded one, and the old one. In mainstream modern Wicca, the God is typically viewed as having dual nature, a god of both light and shadow. In this regard, he represents the waxing and waning periods of Nature.

The horned one is most commonly depicted as a stag-horned god, symbolizing fertility. The stag symbolism relates to protection of the herd. The nature of the dominant stag to fend off other males creates a link to the maiden goddess form. Here we see the horned one as the consort of the maiden.

The hooded one is symbolized by the classic Green Man imagery, but is also depicted as a man of the forest wearing a hooded cloak. The classic Oak King and Holly King are forms of this aspect, although they are not typically viewed in Wicca as being gods. The nature of the lush growth of field and forest creates a link to the mother goddess form. Here we see the hooded one as the consort of the mother.

The old one is symbolized by the wise sage figure, the great elder carrying his staff. He is the most human of forms, and yet is the meeting place between the mortal and divine realms. Unlike the other forms that are connected to the animal and plant kingdoms, the old one represents the union between human and divine consciousness. Here we see wise-man imagery, which creates a connection with the crone goddess form. In this, we find the old one as the consort of the crone.

Cultural Expressions

When we look at the myths and legends of various cultures, we find a commonality of how our ancestors viewed gods and goddesses. The stories that appear in various cultures are flavored by the regional differences, which include climate, terrain, and animal life. For example, the colder regions of northern Europe have different depictions of the gods than does southern Europe. Another example is a culture that is nomadic, versus one that settled in rich agricultural regions. Here we find differences in the tales of gods and goddesses. However, when looking at all of these cultures, we find more similarities than we do differences as a whole.

It is interesting to note that in the character of the deities depicted in myth and legend, we find the nature of the people that worship them. Where resources are more limited and weather is harsh, we find deities that are seemingly stern and aggressive. In regions where the weather is mild and resources are plentiful, we find deities that appear refined and joyful in comparison. It is only natural that our ancestors saw the gods in the same way that they saw their own lives. Here we find that the deities express the needs, desires, and even the fears of the people who worship them.

When selecting a pantheon, it is advisable to think about your own nature and how you might want to strengthen or enhance it. There are two primary approaches to consider. If you tend to be passive but want to be more assertive, then the choice of active and strong deities can help in transforming your nature. However, if you are comfortable with being passive, then as a support you may wish to connect with deities that reflect that nature. So, in this context, your two approaches are to complement or transform.

A Word of Caution

Many people in modern Wicca prefer an eclectic approach when selecting a pantheon. The eclectic view is that just about anything is okay if it works for the individual or group. Over the years, I have seen people use a pantheon comprised of a goddess of love and a god of war, for example Venus and Aries. I have also seen people match deities such as Athena and Aries as a consort pair. But is it wise to create consorts who are not mates in the myths and legends of our ancestors? Is there a practical and noteworthy reason why our ancestors matched and mated certain deities and not others?

Some Wiccans go outside of specific cultures and create consort pairs that are not from the same region. One example is creating a consort pair with an Aegean/Mediterranean goddess and a Celtic god, or vice versa. In choosing this approach, care should be given to understanding the myths and legends of each deity before mating them. This includes looking at the totem animals associated with each in order to be certain that neither deity is offended (remember gods and goddesses have their own likes and dislikes). But you do not need to be concerned about the compatibility of the animal totems, such as a goddess associated with cats and a god associated with wolves. The primary concern is not to include a totem that is specifically referenced as offensive in the myth of any specific deity.

Mating deities from other cultures is especially challenging. For example, creating a consort pair with an African god and Celtic goddess can be problematic. This is because the natures of the deities are rooted in a different tribal consciousness and may not integrate in the same way that deities from European regions might.

Several years ago, I was given a Ganesh statue (an elephant-headed god from Hindu culture). I was looking for a place to set it in my bedroom, and in order to free my hands to prepare an area, I temporarily placed Ganesh on the table where my shrine to Hecate is located. I immediately felt an unpleasant jolt of energy go through me, and an inner voice spoke sharply: "Get that *thing* off my shrine!" It was the voice of Hecate.

The example of Ganesh strongly suggests that it may be more practical to remain within the same cultural roots when creating consorts. Cultural pantheons are energy forms that blend and work well together because they were created in that regard. Mixing and matching pantheons from foreign cultures can be like mixing drugs from different and unrelated family groups. Education and caution is highly recommended in both ventures.

Patron Deities

A patron deity is one that assists and inspires you in some specific way or for a particular venture. In most cases a patron deity involves a less formal relationship than does the primary deity of a tradition. A patron deity may not even require a pre-established schedule of dates for veneration and offerings. It can be as simple as providing an offering whenever you invoke or evoke the deity.

There are several ways to discover your patron deity. One method is to try and find a festival day that honors a particular deity that coincides with your birthday. Explore mythology books and look for deities whose nature calls to you. For example, I was born on the festival day of the goddess Ceres, who is the patron of the Mysteries. Long before I discovered this fact, I had already been drawn to studying the ancient mystery traditions of Greece and Rome. Upon discovering the date connection, I realized that Ceres was my patroness.

Another method for discovering your patron deity is to look for connections to natural talents. For example, if you have always been strongly drawn to music, art, or literature, you may be able to discover associated deities. A list can be found in the chapter on correspondences.

In many cases you will find that a patron deity selects you, as opposed to you having to search one out. This can manifest in several ways. One common experience is to continually encounter tokens or totems associated with a deity. For example, you may continually come across things connected to owls, and then later discover an attraction to a deity represented by an owl. Another means of encountering your patron deity is to be visited by her or him in a dream, meditation, guided imagery journey, or trance state.

Nameless Gods and Goddesses

A final consideration is the use of deity titles as opposed to actual names. The benefit of this approach is that you will not be tied to any specific cultural pantheon. This universal appeal may be helpful for members of a tradition who are widely diverse in their views concerning deities and the cultures from which they originated.

In this section I will present a working model drawn from one of my earlier books, *Witchcraft: A Mystery Tradition.* The basic format includes the concept of a mated pair that journeys together in a common mythology that is marked by the eight Sabbats. The following is a list of deity titles associated with the Sabbats.

Samhain: Lady of Shadows and Lord of Shadows

Yule: Lady of the Womb and Lord of Rebirth

Imbolc: Lady of Fire and Lord of Ice

Ostara: Lady of the Lake and Lord of the Reeds

Beltane: Lady of the Green and Lord of the Green

Litha: Lady of the Flowers and Lord of the Woods

Lughnasadh: Lady of the Fields and Lord of the Barley

Mabon: Lady of the Harvest and Lord of the Sheaf

Let's look at the titles and the themes they express.

The idea of deities within shadow is linked to chthonic nature as well as to a concept beyond the typical classifications of gods and goddesses. For example, in ancient Etruscan mythology a race of beings existed known as the Involuti. These beings were above the so-called high gods who appear in rulership roles. Another example appears in the idea of the Fates who were above the Olympic gods. In Celtic myths we can include the Tuatha De Danaan as deities within the realm of shadow.

In mainstream Wiccan view, the year begins on November Eve with the festival of Samhain. Here we see that the year begins in the darkness of the late fall season. In essence, this is the dark womb experience, from which the waxing year will be ushered in. It is in this time of the year that the Lady and Lord of Shadows rule. Therefore, to this season we can assign deities that are mysterious and magical, and who relate to hidden or secret realms.

The following season is marked by the celebration of Yule. At this time the deity titles are the Lady of the Womb and the Lord of Rebirth. Within this mythos we find the idea of light being born from the darkness. In one sense this is the ancestral view of the sun and the moon rising in the east (seemingly from beneath the earth itself). In this season the deities of birth and regeneration rule.

Next we arrive at the season of Imbolc. The deity titles for this season are the Lady of Fire, and the Lord of Ice. Here we find the world frozen in the grip of winter. The most noticeable aspect of winter is the loss or reduction of vegetation, as well as the appearance of ice and snow. The God, typically being associated with vegetation, is frozen away. It is the Goddess whose passionate flame can thaw and release the god. This season is ruled by the deities associated with potential, and with the power of forging and fire.

The next season is Ostara. The deity titles for this season are the Lady of the Lake and the Lord of the Reeds. Ice and snow have melted away with the warmth of the fire of the Goddess. The God is released from bondage within winter's grasp. In this mythos, we find the return of warmth and the transformation of ice and snow into water. Deities of liberation, release, and fertility are associated with this season (as well as deities associated with planting and with fertile soil).

The following season is Beltane. The deity titles for this season are the Lady of the Green and the Lord of the Green. The combination of warmth and water has brought forth lush vegetation. The Goddess is the Green Lady, and the God is the Green Lord. In this mythos we find the rule of deities associated with return, regrowth, and renewal (all associated with fertile energy).

Next we arrive at Litha. The deity titles for this season are the Lady of Flowers and the Lord of the Woods. The greenery of the last season has grown to enhance the fields and forests. In this mythos, the Lady brings forth the beauty of nature in the flowers and colors of summer. The God is within the animals, trees, and plants of the woodlands.

Deities associated with wildlife and botanicals rule at this season.

The following season is Lughnasadh. The deity names for this season are the Lady of the Fields and the Lord of the Barley. The bounty of nature now looms in ripeness, and the anticipation of the harvest is at hand. In this mythos, the deities of abundance, maturity, and ripeness now rule the season.

Finally, we arrive at the last season, known as Mabon. The deity titles for this season are the Lady of the Harvest, and the Lord of the Sheaf. This season marks the harvesting of nature's bounty and the collecting of seeds for the coming planting season. At this time, the deities of descent, decline, transformation, and mystical journey rule the season.

Now that we have looked at the general theme associated with the seasons and the Sabbats, you have a template for deity natures. By selecting deities whose natures coincide with any given mythos or seasonal theme, you can create a sound pantheon to empower your Wheel of the Year. With this understanding in hand, let us now turn to an examination of the Wheel of the Year itself.

four

WEAVING THE WHEEL
OF THE YEAR

In mainstream Wicca, there are eight celebrations or festivals of the year. They are collectively known as the Wheel of the Year. Symbolically, they are often depicted on an eight-spoke wagon wheel, with each spoke representing one of the eight seasonal rites. In Wicca, the sequence of the seasons is often referred to as the turning of the year. Therefore the Wheel of the Year is symbolic of this natural event.

Most Wiccan traditions include seasonal themes that incorporate the myths and legends of the associated deities. These themes appear in the eight seasonal celebrations of Wicca, which are also known as the Sabbats. The ritual of each Sabbat is built upon the myth or legend of the deities that are associated with that particular season. This is known as a mythos, which is a cohesive and interconnected collection that serves as the foundation for the celebrations of the year.

A well-constructed and blended Wheel of the Year structure will provide for the richness of connection to the *Momentum of the Past*. The momentum of the past is a spiritual current that flows from past generations into contemporary times. This will help vitalize your rituals in ways that will intensify the ritual experience. Therefore, it is beneficial to consider the Wheel of the Year as both a whole unit and a series of connective parts.

For the purposes of this chapter, we will think of the wheel as a complete story. Each of the Sabbats is a chapter in that story. The story is about a goddess and god who are mated. Their relationship and their lives are played out in the unfolding of the seasons of the year. Once you know the theme of each Sabbat (as an expression of the whole), you can then work your deities into the Wheel of the Year format that suits your tradition.

In the mainstream view of modern Wicca, the mythological theme of the Wheel of the Year can be sorted into the following topics:

1. October: Samhain, the beginning of the year awaiting birth in the realm of shadow

2. December: Yule (Winter Solstice), the birth of new light

3. February: Imbolc, the time of purification and preparation

4. March: Ostara (Spring Equinox), the stirring of fertility, the awakening of the seed

5. May: Beltane, the mating of the female and male forces, the impregnation of Nature

6. June: Litha (Summer Solstice) the fullness of Nature's bounty

7. August: Lughnasadh, the harvest or birth of abundance

8. September: Mabon (Autumn Equinox), the decline of the life force into shadow

Most modern traditions incorporate two central themes into the Wheel of the Year. The first is a mated goddess and god consort pair that represents the fertilizing and life-giving forces of Nature. The second theme integrates personifications of the waxing (growing) and waning (declining) forces of Nature, which divide the year into two halves. One half is the season of growth and gain, and the other is the season of decline and loss. One classic example of personification is the Holly King and Oak King figures. Another example is the Stag (waxing) and Wolf (declining) figures, which are primal forces versus human imagery.

The God and Goddess Theme

The most popular mythical theme in modern Wicca is that of a Goddess and God who meet, court, fall in love, and produce an offspring. The Goddess is connected to the moon and the earth. The God is connected to the sun and the earth (although in many traditions he is also the Sky Father, as opposed to being specifically the sun). These themes are further explored in other chapters.

The God is born at Yule where he represents the new sun for the coming year. This theme is quite ancient, and reflects the concept of rebirth and renewal. At Yule, a time when daylight has dwindled, the newborn sun symbolizes the new light that will save the world from darkness. The mother of the newborn Sun God is the Earth Goddess who, at this time, dwells in the Underworld. Just as the sun seems to rise from below the earth, and the seed rises from below the soil, so too is the Sun God birthed from the Earth Mother.

In February, at the time of Imbolc, the Sun God is bound to winter's hold. The Goddess is the flame that begins to thaw and attract the God. At the Spring Equinox (Ostara), the Goddess returns youthful again to the mortal realm from the Underworld, bringing the promise of renewed life. Beltane marks the courtship of the young Sun God with the Divine Maiden.

At the Summer Solstice (Litha), the Goddess and God wed. The seasonal rite of Lughnasadh marks the ripened harvest. The Autumn Equinox (Mabon) features the death of the Sun God as the Harvest Lord, at which time the Goddess descends into the Underworld to retrieve her lover. With the onset of Samhain, the Goddess and God are reunited in the Underworld. The celebration of the Winter Solstice (Yule) marks the renewal of the Wheel of the Year mythos once again.

The God and Goddess in the Wheel of the Year

Over the past few decades many eclectic systems have altered the pre-existing mythos, or have modified it to create something new. This has resulted in many different themes, and it can lead to confusion when re-searching deities and their role in the Wheel of the Year mythos. In this section we will explore some approaches to creating a cohesive storyline upon which to build your own Wheel of the Year deity assignments.

In order to construct a wheel mythos, you will first need to decide in which season to begin your story. As previously mentioned, most mod-ern traditions place the meeting of the Goddess and God at the Spring Equinox. Their courtship begins at May, and the Goddess is visibly preg-nant by Summer Solstice. The God dies in the Fall season (in some tradi-tions this occurs at Lughnasadh, and in others at Mabon). The Goddess and God are reunited in the Underworld at Samhain (November Eve). The Goddess gives birth to their son on the Winter Solstice.

Some confusion exists due to the fact that most contemporary tradi-tions begin the year with the season of Samhain at the close of Octo-ber/beginning of November. In contrast, the Goddess and God meet in the spring. The problem here is that at the time of Samhain she has already been impregnated with child by the God. Therefore, the year ap-parently begins in the middle of the relationship between the Goddess and God. This is only a problem if the chronology bothers your sense of logic.

One way to resolve this is to begin the year in your tradition at the time of the Spring Equinox. Another way is to simply view the year as nonlinear, a circle with no beginning or end. Here Samhain can be viewed as a point within the shadow of the year, a moment in which to begin the mythos in procreative darkness, which moves toward the birthing of light at the Winter Solstice.

Another potential storyline problem exists in the assignment of the crone aspect of the Goddess to the season of Samhain. In most tradi-tions, the Goddess is pregnant at this time of year, which seems to con-flict with the nature of an elderly deity. When we look at the Wheel of the Year as a whole, the aging of the deities from birth is very rapid when compared to the human cycle. Typically, the God is born at Yule, is an adolescent by Imbolc, and a young man by Beltane.

The confusion regarding a pregnant deity who is also the crone aspect of the Goddess is rooted in eclectic creativity. The earlier structure depicted a patroness of the Samhain season, which is now viewed as the crone aspect of the Goddess. Her original role at Samhain was to escort the dead, and this role was simply a manifestation of one of her aspects in connection with the festival celebration. Behind this appearance there also existed the larger mythos, which reflects the Wheel of the Year story (as opposed to a singular festival association). But in the earliest forms of this mythos, the Goddess is not described as old (or of any particular age).

When we look at the contemporary construction of Wicca, we often find the overlapping of myths and legends that originally stood separate and independent from one another. In sorting things out, it is helpful to note the parallel mythos that marks a Sabbat, along with the mythos that turns the Wheel of the Year. One example is the appearance of the Oak King and Holly King at the time of the Summer Solstice and Winter Solstice. They do not appear elsewhere in the Wheel of the Year, and are noted only at the time of two individual Sabbats. Therefore, they are independent tales that do not require reconciliation with the overall mythos of the Sabbats.

The singular appearance of a deity or character signifies the outer layer of a mythos as it relates to the Wheel of the Year. You can picture this like a circle with a ring in the center. The circle represents the Sabbats, and the ring symbolizes the inner mythos of the Wheel of the Year. On the circle, each Sabbat is associated with a deity or mystical character. On the ring the mated pair of deities appears (who travel together throughout the year, see figure 1). In effect, there are two stories being told. One is the tale of individual deities or figures as they appear isolated at specific points in the year. The other story presents the Goddess and God as a couple that is continually depicted together throughout the year.

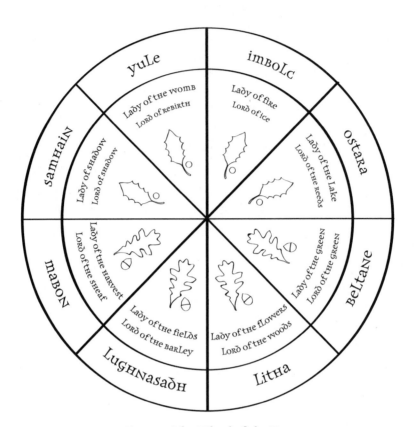

Figure 1: The Wheel of the Year

In Shadow and in Light

When we look at the Sabbats from a traditional perspective a distinct pattern emerges. This pattern depicts the celebration of the Sabbats on dates that alternate between day and night. What we note first is that solar festivals fall on either the day of an equinox or a solstice. These clearly belong to the Sun God and his unique mythos.

The second thing we note is that four of the Sabbats traditionally fall in the evening. For example, May Eve (Beltane) and November Eve (Samhain) are night festivals. Imbolc was traditionally celebrated on the eve of February, and Lughnasadh was traditionally celebrated on August Eve. In modern times this has been changed to daytime celebrations, with Imbolc on or near February 2, and Lughnasadh on August 1. Many modern traditions also celebrate Beltane on the day of May 1, while most traditions appear to still celebrate Samhain at night. If you choose to create your tradition in accord with an older view, then you will want to set your Sabbat dates to reflect day and night.

In the mythos of shadow and light, the Goddess represents all that is associated with the night. Naturally this includes the moon and the stars. Because night obscures things from our sight, it is associated with the hidden, secret, and mystical. Night also represents potentiality, the idea that anything is possible before it can be seen. This is, in part, the notion of magic. In this regard, we can view the eve celebrations as spiritual and conceptual.

In contrast to the eve celebrations, the solar rites are performed beneath the sun. Therefore, the God represents all that is associated with daylight, which includes the sun, blue skies, and clouds. Because daylight reveals everything to our sight, it is associated with the tangible, practical, and commonplace. Daytime also represents safety and protection, the idea that we are forewarned and alerted because of increased visibility. In this regard we can view the daytime celebrations as worldly and detail oriented.

By focusing on the alternating role of the Goddess and God through the year you can separately honor each deity in her or his role. If you choose to adopt this approach, then it is beneficial to highlight the Goddess or God in some special way on the appropriate Sabbat. This can be as simple as decorating the altar statue or incorporating a play in your ritual in which the deity is given offerings or special attention in some appropriate manner.

In order to select offerings, or create rituals to honor the deities, you can research and study the myths and legends of your deity pair. Look for mentions of any food, flowers, or settings that appear in the myth. This will help you select appropriate offerings, and will help you get to know the likes and dislikes of any particular deity. It is also beneficial to note any adventures and special achievements presented in a myth or legend. This will give you ritual text to include in which you can sing the praises of the deity. The deities enjoy a little flattery.

The Waxing and Waning Theme

In modern Wicca, the year is divided into two halves. As mentioned earlier, one half is called the waxing year, which refers to the seasons of growth and gain. The other half is called the waning year, which refers to decline and loss. Some traditions mark these shifts at the Summer and Winter Solstice days. Other traditions mark them at the shifts occurring on the Spring Equinox and Autumn Equinox.

In many Wiccan systems the Holly King assumes power at the Summer Solstice, and his reign brings the decline of Nature into fall and winter. The Oak King assumes power at the Winter Solstice, and his reign ushers in the season of growth and abundance in Nature (spring and summer). In some systems the stag assumes power at the Spring Equinox, and the wolf does the same at the Fall Equinox. Like the Oak King and Holly King, these entities initiate the changing of the seasons that mark the waxing and waning periods.

If you want to include the theme of the waxing and waning halves of the year, then you can add the personifications of your choice into your ritual structure. This can be as simple as decorating the altar or ritual area with images of the Holly and Oak King, or the Stag and the Wolf. The old-fashioned Santa figures at Christmas time are ideal, and you can select them in accord with the objects and seasonal foliage carried by any given figure. The dark-clothed Santa figures (greens and browns) can serve as the Oak King, and the lighter-clothed figures (reds and whites) make a nice Holly King. Figurines of a stag and a wolf can be found throughout the year.

Another way of acknowledging the waxing and waning forces is to perform a ritual drama in costume. Decide whether you want to mark the waxing and waning periods on the equinox or solstice celebrations. Accordingly, you can choose the figures you want to represent the waxing and waning forces (and of course, the drama includes the resulting victory of one over the other).

Mock battles have been part of the tradition of ritual for many centuries. This is the classic struggle of "good" and "evil" as perceived by humankind. However, in Nature such things do not exist, and there is only the cycle of birth, growth, maturity, decline, and death. The interpretation of good and evil is subjective, not objective.

The Altar and the Wheel of the Year

The altar can be viewed as the focal point of the ritual proceedings, and as such it can be decorated to represent the central theme of the season. In addition to the décor, it is advisable to set on it the connective icons and symbols that connect to the essence of your tradition. This is where your tradition will come together in symbolism and representation, which will allow the participants to connect on deeper levels with what is displayed on the altar.

Ideally, the altar is placed in the direct center of the ritual circle. In this way, the directional points of north, east, south, and west cross and meet on the center of the altar. This becomes the sacred area of the altar. Therefore, you will want to think about setting something special in this area. In my tradition, we place the spirit flame, which is a lighted bowl of high-grade alcohol (such as 180 proof) on the altar. The flame represents the living and nonpersonified presence of divinity. For yourself, you may instead want to place a special crystal to catch and focus the quarter's emanations.

Upon the altar place statues or representations of the Goddess and God. Think about what position on the altar is most symbolic for you. In my tradition, we place the Goddess on the left and the God on the right. These positions represent electrical (right) and magnetic (left). They are symbolic of the masculine and feminine polarities in standard occultism. You can use symbolic placement or not—as you wish.

To complete the altar, as an operative center, set representations of the four creative elements: earth, air, fire, and water. In my tradition, we use small bowls that contain a representation. You can place soil in the earth bowl, incense in the air bowl, a votive candle for fire, and some spring water in the water bowl. In effect, these representations are the battery for the creative forces that aid you in casting your ritual or magical circle.

Now that you have the core established, the next step is to place the operative tools. These include your candles, incense holder, snuffer, cutting blade, cords, and whatever else you may need. To complete the altar's functionality, you will want to set your ritual tools in place as well. Traditionally, these are the pentacle, wand, athame, and chalice.

The final stage is to decorate the altar with seasonal themes. In this regard, think of the plants, fruits, grains, and flowers that are traditional symbols of the season. For example, pumpkins and gourds are typical for the fall season. Flowers can be used for the summer, and seeds and bulbs are ideal for spring. For winter, the traditional holly and pinecones are good choices. As a final touch, add colored candles to symbolize the feel of the season.

Now that we have looked at the Wheel of Year and its essential aspects, we can turn our attention to constructing the rituals of a tradition. In the next chapter we will explore creating rituals and look at some functional models to consider. Turn to the next chapter and let's move deeper into crafting Wiccan traditions.

five

CREATING RITUALS

In previous chapters we have looked at the aspects of creating a tradition and selecting a pantheon. In this chapter we will examine the process of creating rituals that express the connection of the pantheon to the tradition. A ritual structure built around a pantheon brings a cohesive and empowering component to the rites of the tradition.

Within most traditions there are two primary types of ritual. One is of a religious or spiritual nature, and the other is of a magical nature. The primary purpose of a religious rite is to participate in the relationship with the pantheon, which includes veneration and the placing of offerings. Magical rites are typically designed to request aid in a variety of matters, to raise energy for protection or healing, or to resolve conflicts.

One ancient idea is that what happens to the deity eventually happens to its followers. In the ancient mystery traditions, this included the theme of death and resurrection. This is also an aspect of Christianity as seen in the mythos of Jesus dying and rising from the dead, which is a very old Pagan theme. Ritual can help to create alignments to deity that unite us with its essence. Through this, the soul is carried in the cycle or flowing stream of the divine emanation. In other words, to align with a god who is born, dies, and returns is to place the soul in the same pattern and current of energy.

Ritual magic is the idea that nonmaterial forces can create changes or manifestations in the material world. This type of magic requires a formula with specific procedures, techniques, and applications. Such a system is believed to make it possible to attract or raise energy that can be condensed, contained, and directed in accord with the desired effect. This energy is attracted, amplified, and directed through the means of a ritual or magical circle large enough to contain the practitioners.

Let's look at a couple of models for creating a work circle. From these you can get an idea about the type of circle you want and what you need to create one for your tradition.

Circle Models

The role of the circle is to map out the ritual area, to contain the energy raised within it, and to protect the inhabitants from contrary forces that might appear in the setting. The traditional model for a Wiccan circle is a marked-out area at least eighteen feet in diameter. In the center an altar is placed, upon which sit the ritual tools and required items for the rite. Along the edge of the circle, at the cardinal points, a candle or torch is set to mark the north, east, south, and west quarters.

The four creative elemental forces of earth, air, fire, and water are evoked in order to establish a sphere of energy that will enclose the entire circle (including top and bottom). In essence, the elemental forces maintain the integrity of the sphere during the ritual. In order to dissolve the sphere, the elemental forces must be released so that they return to their natural and separate states of existence. The withdrawal of the elements will automatically dissolve the energy sphere.

In mainstream Wicca, it is common to evoke the circle guardians to the four quarters. This is usually done after the circle is established with the elemental forces. Many traditions call upon the guardians, beginning with the east quarter and then moving clockwise around to the east again. In some traditions the evocations are begun at the north, and they also continue in a clockwise manner. Traditionally the guardians are released in a counterclockwise fashion.

Customarily, the Wiccan circle is declared to be cast following its ritual establishment. Once the ritual is completed, then the circle is released and a declaration made that it is dissolved. This affirms the circle's status in both the material and astral realms. In this way, no undesired residual energy is left behind from the ritual itself.

Now that we have reviewed the basic idea of constructing a circle, let's turn our attention to looking at a couple of functional models.

Example One: Circle Casting

1. Preparation: On your altar consecrate the salt and water by mixing a pinch of salt in a small container of purified water, saying:

   I consecrate this water with salt, and thereby cast out all that is negative and contrary to my intent.

2. Sprinkle the consecrated salt water around the ritual area where the circle will be cast.

3. Mark out the ritual area for the circle on the ground with rope, stones, or candles.

4. Evocation of the four elements: Place representations of the four elements on the altar (for example, soil for earth, incense smoke for air, a votive candle for fire, and a cup of water for water). Earth is the north position, air in the east, fire in the south, and water in the west. Place the palm of the left hand over each of the elements (beginning with earth and moving clockwise) and say:

   I call between the worlds and evoke the element of _____ to be present in this time and place.

5. Charge athame (or sword): Touch the tip of the blade to each elemental substance (beginning with earth and moving clockwise), saying:

   I charge this blade with the creative element of _____, that it may be a tool through which I establish my will and intent.

6. Trace over the circle with the athame (or sword), saying:
   I conjure this circle to be a place between the worlds, which
   shall contain the power raised within. I consecrate this circle
   as a barrier and a protection against all that is contrary to
   my will and intent.

7. Return to the altar and affirm:
   In the names of the Goddess and the God, I declare the circle
   has been established.

8. Evoke the Guardians by going to each of the directional quarters
   (beginning east and moving clockwise) and presenting the pentagram of evocation. Following the tracing of the pentagram in
   the air, say:
   Please hear me, Old Ones, Guardians of the circle between
   the worlds. I summon, stir, and call you forth to be witness to
   the rites performed herein.

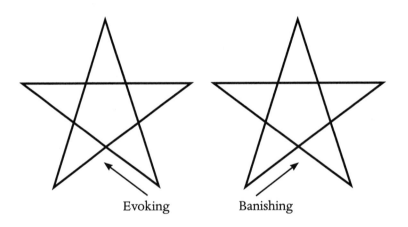

Evoking   Banishing

Figure 2: Evocational Pentagram
(old traditional, not Golden Dawn tradition)

9. Return to the altar and declare the circle to be fully cast.

10. Once the ritual is complete, bid farewell to the guardians in reverse order, and then release the elements at the altar bowls (also
in reverse order of the evocation). To do so, simply thank the entities for attending the ritual, bow, and say, "Fare thee well," or
similar words.

In this first model of circle casting, we are looking at the basic structure of establishing or casting a circle. As demonstrated in the ritual, the
four elements are evoked in order to provide the building materials of
creation. These elemental qualities are drawn into the athame, which
is then used to direct the element forces into the creation of a ritual or
magical circle. The presence of the elemental forces (temporarily bound
to their representations on the altar) feeds the elemental energy fields
that comprise the circle. They form and maintain a sphere of energy
that encloses the ritual area, with the circle and altar sealed inside.

The magnetic properties that bind the elemental forces together in
the circle's sphere also record the spoken, visualized, and willed intent
of the ritualist who cast the circle. This is not unlike the principles that
allow magnetic strips of tape to record voices and music on a cassette,
or data that becomes stored on a magnetic disk. This is at work in the
ritual as the evocational calls are sounded to *conjure* the intent of the
circle. In model one, this intent is to contain energy and to protect from
the intrusion of any energy that is contrary to the nature of the ritual.

Following the completion of the circle casting, the circle is declared
established in the names of the Goddess and God. This is, in essence,
the invocation of deity, which breathes life into the circle and brings the
elements into harmony. This is reflected in the occult principle that the
fifth element of spirit governs the interaction of the four elements of
earth, air, fire, and water.

The final stage of casting the circle in model one depicted the evocation of the guardians or watchers. As previously noted, the watchers fall
into the category of stellar beings that exert influence upon the earth.
This is a very old and basic concept that can be seen in the astral magic

systems of ancient Mesopotamia. In the Babylonian system there were four stars known as the Royal Watchers. It is an old belief that stars influence the nature and destiny of humans. Today we see this principle operative in the system of astrology and the horoscope. In this sense, we can say that the watchers exert influence over the ritual circle and the proceedings within it.

As seen in the circle model, once a ritual is completed the guardians/watchers and elementals need to be released to return back to their domains. In addition to being sound ritual and magic, it is also simple courtesy. With the withdrawal of these entities, the sphere dissolves away and the circle shifts back from between the worlds.

The following model for circle casting is very similar, except that it involves a deeper level of incorporating the elemental forces. Look it over and see which model you prefer. As always, you can modify the material in this book or create something entirely different. The value of what is presented lies in its foundational material, which you can build upon.

Example Two: Circle Casting

1. Mark out the ritual area for the circle on the ground with rope, stones, or candles.

2. Light altar candles at each of the circle quarters: north, east, south, west.

3. Consecrate water: On your altar, consecrate the salt and water by mixing in a pinch of salt to a small container of purified water, saying:

   I exorcise thee, O creature of water, that thou cast out from thee all impurities and uncleanliness of the spirits of the world of the phantasm. In the names of the Goddess and God, so mote it be.

4. Evocation of the four elements: Place representations of the four elements on the altar (soil for earth, incense smoke for air, a votive candle for fire, and a cup of water for water). Earth is the

north position, air in the east, fire in the south, and water in the west. Place the palm of the left hand over each of the elements (beginning with earth and moving clockwise) and say:

I call between the worlds and evoke the element of _____
to be present in this time and place.

5. Draw the elements: Take each of the elemental representations around the circle, starting at the associated quarter (returning to the quarter and then moving to the altar).

Air—starting at the east, carry smoking incense and say:
In the beginning the thought moved out into nothingness and
filled the void.

Fire—starting at the south, carry a lighted candle and say:
And into the misty void burned the desire for creation.

Water—starting at the west, carry a container of water and say:
Then from within the flame of desire poured forth movement
and direction.

Earth—starting at the north, carry the earth representation and say:
And from movement and direction there arose substance, and
so did manifestation take root.

Return to the altar.

6. Charge athame (or sword): Touch the tip of the blade to each elemental substance (beginning with earth and moving clockwise), saying:

I charge this blade with the creative element of _____, *that*
it may be a tool through which I establish my will and intent.

7. Trace over the circle with the athame (or sword), saying:
I conjure this circle to be a place between the worlds, which
shall contain the power raised within. I consecrate this circle
as a barrier and a protection against all that is contrary to
my will and intent.

8. Return to the altar and affirm:

    In the names of the Goddess and the God, I declare the circle
    has been established.

9. Evoke the guardians by going to each of the directional quarters
    (beginning east and moving clockwise) and presenting the pen-
    tagram of evocation. Following the tracing of the pentagram in
    the air, say:

    Please hear me, Old Ones, Guardians of the circle between
    the worlds. I summon, stir, and call you forth to be witness to
    the rites performed herein.

10. Return to the altar and declare the circle to be fully cast.

11. Once the ritual is complete, bid farewell to the guardians in re-
    verse order, and then release the elements at the altar bowls (also
    in reverse order of the evocation). To do so, simply thank the en-
    tities for attending the ritual, bow, and say, "I fare thee well" (or
    similar words).

In addition to the circle models, there are other associated models to
consider as well. The three primary models to explore are the lunar,
solar, and Sabbat models. These will help you decide how to structure
your ritual themes in order to create the most effective alignments to
your tradition.

Lunar Models

The role of the moon is both magical and spiritual. Rituals associated
with the moon are designed to align with, and interface with, the various phases of the moon. Each phase emanates a specific type of energy
that can be tapped to enhance a work of magic or ritual intent. There
are four basic lunar models to work with: dark moon, waxing moon,
full moon, waning moon.

Traditionally the dark moon is the three days in which the moon cannot be seen. To this phase belong chthonic themes, shamanic journeys,
ancestral veneration, and things of an occult nature. When we read tales

of cauldrons hidden in a dungeon or in the depths of the Underworld (or Otherworld), this is the time of the dark moon journey. When working with dark moon energy, it is effective to include ritual items such as jet and amber, black candles, black clothing, earthy incense, and dark wine.

The waxing phase of the moon is beneficial for rituals intended for gain, prosperity, increase, improved health, and general good fortune. Traditionally the waxing period begins after the last night of the dark moon (with the first appearance of the crescent). Waxing moon rituals are well served by incorporating green candles, sweet incense, light-colored clothing (if any), and white wine.

The night of the full moon is traditionally the time of magic and mystical events. Works of magic and ritual intentions are amplified when the moon is full. The full moon is also among the highly favored times to venerate the deities of the moon and stars. It is also a good time for ancestral veneration. For good results, include silver- and white-colored items, camphor-based incense, and offerings of red wine and grain cakes or cookies.

The waning phase of the moon is best for rituals and spells that are intended to dissolve, separate, or dissipate. It is also traditionally the time of dark magic intended to cause harm or ill (specifically in terms of retribution or revenge). In modern Wicca this is viewed as inappropriate in keeping with the Wiccan Rede, which states that no intended harm may come from the design or function of any ritual or spell.

In addition to the phases of the moon, a classic lunar model is what's commonly referred to as Drawing Down the Moon. In mainstream Wicca, this refers to invoking the consciousness of the Goddess into the body of a priestess or a high priestess. It is believed that this makes it possible for the Goddess to speak directly through the human vessel. Drawing Down the Moon is most often performed at the time of the full moon.

A variant on Drawing Down the Moon is the idea that the light or energy of the moon can be directed into a vessel. The light and energy of the moon is considered to be magical. It can be condensed and amplified once it is drawn and collected. This is often performed by using a mirror to reflect the light of the moon onto or into an object. It can also be used to channel the moon's light and energy into a person.

The purpose of lunar rites is to incorporate the spiritual associations of the moon with the subtle energies of the moon's radiations. When incorporating the lunar element into your rituals, think in terms of ways to use the moon's light. One very old tradition used a mirror to direct the light, and others used a bowl of water to catch the reflection of the moon. The moon's light can be used to bless or charge ritual items, charms, or even the ritual participants.

When incorporating spiritual elements into your ritual, think in terms of goddess imagery. Symbols such as white shells, round cakes, ripe fruit, and silver decorations are ideal for lunar associations. The inclusion of a cauldron to represent the womb of the Goddess is a very useful tool. Offerings can be set around it, and petitions on small pieces of parchment can be placed into the cauldron. See the chapter on initiation for an example of the religious, mystical, and sacred aspects of ritual construction.

Solar Models

While Wicca is essentially a lunar-based system, it does indeed possess significant solar aspects as well. The God figure in Wicca is represented and symbolized by the sun. In mainstream Wicca, the journey of the sun throughout the year is personified in the mythos of the God as this relates to the seasons of the year. As noted previously, the solar rites are highlighted by the equinox and solstice days as well as the midpoints of the year that fall exactly between them, the eight Sabbats of the Wiccan Wheel of the Year.

The year is divided into two halves: waxing and waning. These can be viewed as representative of the Lord of Light and the Lord of Darkness, which are the duality of the God's nature. In this respect he is the Sky Father of the bright day sky and the Underworld Lord when his light descends beneath the earth, leaving darkness to cover the land.

Solar-based rituals include ritual items such as yellow candles, grain, stag antlers, and something gold colored to represent the sun. Musical instruments such as the flute and harp can be incorporated into the rites. These types of items enhance the solar vibration and help create the required magical and spiritual alignments that evoke and invoke solar energy.

The purpose of the solar elements is to bring balance and support to the feminine lunar connections. This complimentary energy creates a stable polarity, which enhances the energy for both female and male practitioners in the circle. Incense made with frankincense and cinnamon is ideal for solar alignments. During the waning half of the year add myrrh, which symbolizes the death of the Lord of Light.

Sabbat Models

The role of the Sabbat is celebratory and also serves to align us with the energy of Nature at any given season. The Sabbat tells a story of the Goddess and God, which follows them throughout the year. In this story their relationship is reflective of the process of Nature as well as the journey of the soul through life and death within the material realm. It is ideal to create or establish a story that flows without interruptions to the plot or disappearances of key characters.

Other chapters of this book deal with the Sabbats in greater detail, and for this reason I will only touch on a few important elements here. Remember that there are two parallel stories taking place in the Wheel of the Year. In effect, the stories alternate back and forth like two people singing a duet. Therefore, continuing with the metaphor, two songs are being sung together as one. This is noted in the fact that the festivals aligned to the God are marked by daytime celebrations on the equinox and solstice. The festivals aligned to the Goddess are celebrated on the eve times of the dates that fall exactly in between each of the equinox and solstice days.

The central theme of the Wheel of the Year is the idea that the God is the life force and the energy of impregnation. He is intimately linked to the sun and to its light. In association with this, he is connected to the agricultural year, which is dependent upon the sun's light. By contrast, the Goddess is the vessel of life and the energy of regeneration. She is intimately linked to the moon and its light. In association with this, she is connected to the phases of the moon, the fertile essence, and to death and rebirth (for which the changing form of the moon is strongly linked).

The courtship of the sun and the moon appears in many old tales. In essence this focuses on the rising and setting of the two lights at different times. The moon, being more mysterious in nature, is often the alluring figure. The sun, being less complicated in nature, is often the figure that is attracted and pursues.

Because the light and the warmth of the sun diminish during the year, the associated God is depicted as declining in strength and passing away. The moon, however, remains the same throughout the year in each month's appearance. Therefore, in her myths she never dies. She does, however, journey into the Underworld to retrieve the descended God and to return his vitality through rebirth. These two primary themes should be maintained and incorporated into your tradition's mythos for the Wheel of the Year. Let's look at an overview of the separate, yet related, stories of the Goddess and God in the Wheel of the Year.

Her Story

In the mythos of the Goddess we find two stories. In one, the Goddess is connected to the moon and, in the other story she is connected to the earth. These are the Moon Goddess cycle and the Earth Goddess cycle. Each of them expresses the presence and interaction of the divine feminine.

In the Moon cycle we see the Goddess as comprised of four natures, each one associated with the phases of the moon: dark moon, waxing moon, full moon, and waning moon.

In the dark moon is the Goddess of Shadow and the Otherworld or Underworld. She is the essence of magic itself, and is sometimes called the enchantress. Because she is unseen during the three nights in which

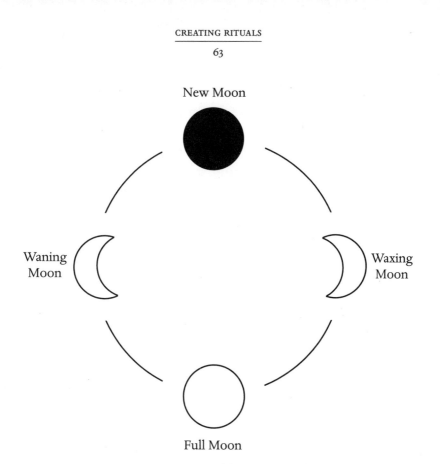

Figure 3: Moon Goddess Cycle Model

the moon is not visible, this aspect of the Goddess is often not noted in modern Wicca. Instead, the mainstream traditions view the Goddess as comprised only of three aspects related to the waxing moon, full moon, and waning moon. We know these aspects as the classic maiden, mother, and crone.

The general story of the Moon cycle Goddess tells us that she dwells in the Underworld. She rises nightly on the eastern horizon from her abode into the world of mortal kind. In the night sky, she drifts gently overhead and then returns to the Underworld at the western horizon. The Moon Goddess gives light to the darkness and emanates her fertile energies, which regulate the menstrual cycles of women. She breathes the essence of magic from the light that falls upon the earth. Through the repeating cycles of the moon, the Goddess teaches us that all life exists with a cycle of birth, maturity, decline, and death. But death is not the end; instead, it is the beginning of the next repeating cycle of life. In this teaching we find the connection to fate.

In ancient times, the Fates were depicted as three women. One was a young maiden, another was a mature woman, and the third was elderly. In essence, they depicted the three stages of life: youth, maturity, and old age. It is easy to see here the basic concept of maiden, mother, and crone. The symbols of the Fates included a spindle, a spinning wheel, and a pair of scissors. The Fates were the daughters of Nox, the goddess of night. In the book *New Cyclopedia*, by J. M. Good, we read this verse: "Them the Fates shall summon, of whom this beauteous maiden, the Moon, is one" (published by T. Davison, 1913).

The ancient philosopher Plutarch, in his essay *The Face in the Orb of the Moon*, wrote that the souls of the departed abide for a time in the paradise of the moon. It is in such themes that we encounter the spiritual role of the Moon Goddess and her connection as the birth-giver of souls. The connection between departed souls and a witchcraft goddess is reflected also in the role of Hecate at the crossroads. In ancient times, the crossroads were believed to be the gathering place of souls unable to find rest or to find their way to the Otherworld/Underworld.

When constructing rituals with lunar themes, think in terms of the mysteries of birth, life, death, and rebirth. Incorporating lunar themes and imagery into initiation rituals is effective. This is covered in the chapter on initiation in this book.

The second model of the Goddess to consider is the Earth Goddess cycle. In this model the Goddess is more tangible and less esoteric than she appears in the Moon cycle model. The primary festivals that mark the Goddess are Samhain, Imbolc, Beltane, and Lughnasadh. At Samhain, she descends into the Underworld, or parts the veil and enters into the Otherworld, in search of her departed mate. At Imbolc, she liberates him from the frozen embrace of winter. By Beltane, the Goddess appears renewed as a young maiden. She is pregnant during the time of Lughnasadh and gives birth to fruit and grain.

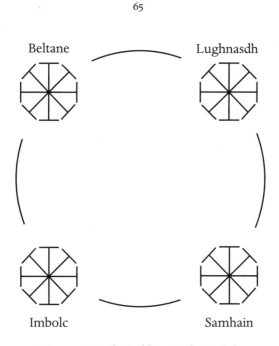

Beltane   Lughnasdh

Imbolc   Samhain

Figure 4: Earth Goddess Cycle Model

When we look at the entire Wheel of the Year mythos we note the addition of the solar story in relationship to the solar festivals, which unite the Goddess with the God on much deeper levels. The Earth Goddess cycle tells the story of a maiden who appears in the spring. She rises from the Underworld or Otherworld and enters the realm of mortal kind, bringing with her the emanation of new life.

As the story continues, the Goddess arrives at May Day, which marks her courtship with the fertile young Lord of Nature. It is through their courtship that the bounty of life returns and is sustained for another year. This theme is most dramatically marked by the marriage and impregnation of the Goddess, which manifests with the Summer Solstice. Here the Earth Goddess is ripe with the bounty of nature.

At Lughnasadh the Goddess is visibly pregnant with the harvest, and she gives birth to the harvest, which is gathered at Mabon. The festival of Mabon marks the death of the Harvest Lord and his descent into the Underworld or Otherworld. As previously noted, the Goddess departs the mortal realm and journeys to find him. They meet in the realm of shadows on Samhain, at which time the Goddess is once again impregnated. The fruit of this union is the newborn Sun God (the Child of Promise), who is born on the Winter Solstice. At this time the Earth Goddess becomes the Great Mother in the divine sense, as opposed to the Great Mother of Nature at the time of Lughnasadh.

When constructing rituals with Earth Goddess themes, think in terms of the seasonal shifts and agricultural symbolism. Incorporating themes associated with fertility and imagery associated with seeds, fruits, and general bounty is important to cohesive ritual structure related to the goddess model.

His Story

In the mythos of the God, we find two related stories. These stories fall into the categories of the Sun God cycle model, and the Harvest Lord cycle model. In the first, the God is connected to the sun, and in the other story, he is connected to the earth. Each model expresses the presence and interaction of the divine masculine.

In the Sun cycle, we see the God as comprised of two natures, each one associated with the two phases of the year. These are the waxing and waning halves marked by the equinox and solstice periods. In the Sun God story, he is the light and warmth that encourages and sustains growth and life in the mortal world. It is for this reason that his myths pivot on the equinox and solstice days, as these are the clearest markers of the solar changes of the year.

Upon examining the Sun God cycle, we note that it begins with the birth of the God at the Winter Solstice. Here, at this time of diminished light and warmth in the material world, the newborn deity is the promise of renewal and return. As the myth continues, the God appears as a youthful man at the Spring Equinox, where he begins his courtship with the Spring Goddess. With the arrival of the Summer Solstice, we find the God wed, and his wife is with child. On the Autumn Equinox, the God begins his journey into the Underworld or Otherworld, leaving behind him the cooling season and the coming increase of darkness.

Yule / Winter Solstice

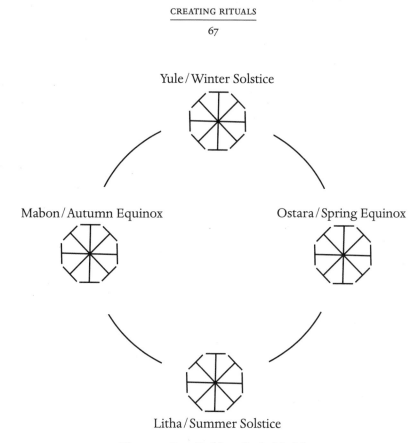

Mabon / Autumn Equinox

Ostara / Spring Equinox

Litha / Summer Solstice

Figure 5: Sun Goddess Cycle Model

When we blend this model with that of the Earth Goddess cycle, the entire story unfolds to a grander view. It is here that we can come to a better understanding of the Goddess and God as a mated pair that interact throughout the Wheel of the Year. There is but one other aspect to add in order to see the whole picture, and this is the story of the Harvest Lord.

The Harvest Lord is a solar-based deity, but with a simpler mythos that is related to the earth as opposed to the sky. In this model, the Harvest Lord reflects the cycle of plant life. This became an important element of life for humankind as it shifted from a hunter-gatherer society to an agrarian society dependent upon cultivated crops.

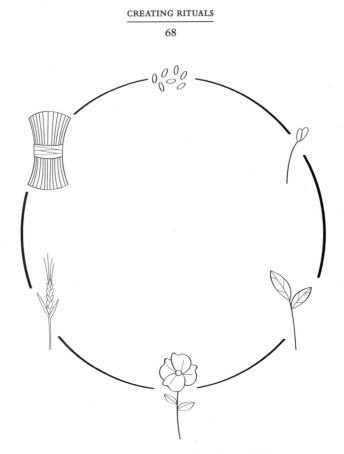

Figure 6: Harvest Lord Cycle Model

The agricultural model of the God begins with the seed, which is the God in the Underworld, where he waits in the darkness of procreation. His birth is signaled by the first sprouts that break the surface of the soil. Here is the fragile infant whose inner power is yet to shine forth in its greatness. The first appearance of leaves is the symbolic herald of the Harvest Lord of the cultivated lands.

The presentation of buds on the plants and trees signals the growing fertile powers of the Harvest Lord. The above display of flowers depicts him in the full array of his vitality. With the appearance of fruit and grain, the Harvest Lord is at the peak of his full power. This phase is followed by his decline, and his death is symbolized by the gathered sheaf. From the harvest is collected the seeds for the next season, which become the first and last symbols of the Harvest Lord, his birth and his death in the endless cycle. You can also use fall leaves on the altar to symbolize decline.

When incorporating elements of the Harvest Lord cycle into your ritual, think in terms of the symbols that represent the life phases. Select the phase that best suits the intent or theme of your ritual. Once selected, use the representations (seeds, flowers, sheaves, etc.) on the altar as decorations or focal points. For the Sun God cycle, do the same and take note of the symbolism appropriate to the waxing and waning forces. Frankincense is ideal for the waxing lord and an incense of myrrh is ideal for the waning lord.

Ritual Components and Structure

Now that we have looked at various models for constructing rituals around a theme, we can examine the practical elements of constructing and empowering rituals. To understand this better, we need to consider two primary aspects. These are the ritual tools and the steps to creating a cohesive and functional ritual. In another chapter, we will also explore the metaphysical aspects that require our attention.

Let's begin with a look at ritual circles. In essence, a circle represents the cosmology of the tradition. In other words, it is constructed and understood along the lines of the internal beliefs and concepts of the tradition in which it appears. Therefore, within the circle rituals of the tradition we should expect to find something reflecting the ideas of divinity, sacred directions, elemental energies, guardians, and so forth. This is often represented on the altar and at the four directional quarters. For example, the altar is set with deity statues, representations of the four elements, and tools by which divinity and the elemental forces are focused and directed within the circle. The most common tools are the traditional pentacle, wand, athame, and chalice.

The use of ritual tools aids in the arousal of altered states of consciousness. Altered states are required for the most effective rituals. In

ancient times this was accomplished through the round dances and inges-
tion of an intoxicating drink or substance. In modern circles, the most
common method is through the personal will and mental imagery.

The process of altering consciousness within a ritual often begins
with chanting. The participating members are led in a chant by a central
figure at the altar. The members move around the circle as the chant
continues, gradually speeding up in tempo. The members do not know
when the chant will cease, which frees the mind to the experience itself.
The end of the chant will be signaled abruptly by the director at the
altar. This act releases the accumulated energy into the circle, which the
coven members have raised through dance and chant.

Moving within a circular motion (in essence through the earth's
magnetic field) causes subtle shifts of electrical energy within the physical bodies of the dancers. This intensifies the aura of each member, and
as energy is raised through dance, each person passes through the raised
accumulative energy field of the coven. You can imagine this as a vapor
trail through which all members move together. This unites each person
and joins them to the group mind of the coven.

Among the most effective ways to raise energy through dancing is to
have the members hold hands and equally distance themselves from one
another. To increase the raised energy, the dance rhythm is designed to
include the shuffling of feet across the ground, which is then followed by
a stomping action (and then the shuffling is repeated again, and so on).
Create your own rhythms and tempos through experimentation. One
suggestion is: shuffle, shuffle, shuffle, shuffle, stomp, stomp, stomp—
stomp, stomp, stomp—shuffle, shuffle, shuffle, shuffle, stomp, stomp,
stomp, etc. Another effective method is to slip-slide the feet across the
ground instead of shuffling. This is similar to the way kids often "skate"
with socks on a slippery floor, but with shorter movements. Naturally,
you will want to fashion a dance step that is more appropriate to the
dignity of a ritual setting.

During the dancing phase, the members need to maintain the chant,
which is directed by the person at the altar. Any changes or additions to
the chant are called out by the director as the chorus nears its end. This

allows the dancers to prepare and join in on the new or added verse. For example, if a chant included a series of goddess names, then the director can call out another name to be chanted as the original verse draws close to being repeated again. This will then change the next verse over to the new goddess name without breaking the tempo of the chant.

The dancers need to retain awareness of the boundaries of the ritual circle. There are two reasons to honor the confines of the ritual circle, and to not step outside of it during the proceedings. The first reason is because to do so breaks connection with the inner cosmos of the circle itself, which spins the person away from the center of what is empowering the ritual. This, in turn, severs the intimate connection between the coven members, which affects the group mind. This is because, in essence, the circle is like a solar system and the members are like planets in orbit around the sun. When one leaves the orbit, the gravitational fields of all are affected.

The second reason for not leaving the circle during a ritual is the energy field itself. The circle is, in essence, an astral barrier. Passing your astral body (which is attached to your physical body) through an astral barrier is like jumping through a glass window. Injuries are likely, and in the case of the astral body, may not show up for several days or weeks, when it can manifest as illness.

There are two ways to avoid damage when exiting a circle. One is to not cast a circle but instead to create sacred space. This is a blessed and consecrated area, as opposed to a formally established ritual circle. The second way to avoid damage is to create a doorway in the circle. While this eliminates injury, it still separates the person leaving from the centrifugal force at the center of the circle.

We should bear in mind that a properly constructed ritual circle crosses between the worlds. In other words, it meshes with other dimensions, and in this regard is like an environmental sphere that supports our needs as living beings. It is wise not to leave the deep sea diving suit while in the depths of the sea. Sacred space is more of a personal agreement about the ritual setting and therefore does not present the metaphysical constraints of a cast circle. However, it also does not provide the same protections and occult benefits.

Another component of the ritual circle is the altar. We have already addressed the altar here in this chapter, but it is important to note its central theme. The altar is, in essence, the hub of the wheel of the circle. It is the direct spiritual center where we meet and interface with divinity. Traditionally, coven members bow at the altar as they enter the ritual circle as a sign of veneration to its principle. A deeper tradition is to place a kiss upon the altar or upon an agreed symbol placed upon the altar. The importance of the ritual kiss is described in the chapter on initiation. You may wish to consider whether to include the traditional honoring of the altar in your tradition or whether you prefer to view it as a work table. I highly recommend the former choice.

When setting the altar, you can create its layout in accord with the traditional occult mythos of creation. To do so, place a black cloth over the altar to represent the darkness of procreation from which all things issue forth. In this darkness of outer space, set a candle to represent the presence of divinity burning at the center of the void. Next place candles or statues to represent the Goddess and God as personifications of the divinity (the central light). At this stage, you will have depicted the Goddess and God overseeing the forthcoming process of creation.

The next stage is to establish the four elements of creation, which in ancient myth were in chaos within the void. According to the ancient tale, spirit (the fifth element) brought the elements into harmony so that creation could take place through their joined properties. You can serve as the hand of harmonizing spirit by arranging the elemental representations of earth, air, fire, and water on your altar. Pass your hand over the center candle flame to connect with the purity of the divine, and then set the elemental representations in place according to their quarterly associations of north, east, south, and west. You can, of course, choose not to adhere to tradition, in which case you will want to think about what the altar represents or means to you. From there, you can set up the altar as you feel is most appropriate for your tradition.

As noted earlier, it is from the altar that the process of casting a circle begins with the elemental connections. What we need to consider next is the invocation of an altered state of consciousness as we create the ritual circle. One effective method is to shift your consciousness as you walk the circle, aligning yourself to each of the four quarters as you approach and pass them.

One method of creating alignments is to visualize the guardian of the directional quarter as you approach it. For example, at the north you can visualize an earthy grotto, feeling inwardly the cool rock and the smell of primal earth. As you take this imagery into your spirit, you can visualize the appearance of a guardian that is appropriate to such a setting. Ideally you should, at this stage, speak or chant the name of the guardian. This will help evoke its presence to the circle and invoke it within your consciousness as well.

It is effective to create a drawing or painting for each guardian image so that there exists a group-mind visualization for the members of your tradition. This imagery will help feed and strengthen the presence of the guardians, creating a powerful group consciousness. But bear in mind that such images are not fantasy characters of the imagination. Instead, they become vessels in which real sentient beings of the Otherworld can manifest in the material realm.

As you walk the circle, repeat an alignment specific to the guardian of each quarter. In this way you are establishing the inner and outer cosmos of your ritual circle, which is a mini-universe representing the tradition's view of creation and its intelligent forces. A circle constructed in this way will enhance the group mind and bring powerful energy to your rituals.

With the formation of the altered state of consciousness, it is effective to affirm the visualized sphere of the ritual circle. To do this, you can use incense smoke. Simply tread the circle and affirm the boundary lines by stating them out loud. Be sure to include above and below along with the edge of the circle itself. For example, you can say, "Here I mark the boundary of the circle's edge," as you pass along the perimeter of the circle. After this you can say, "Here I mark the boundary of that which is above," as you lift the censer up to pass the smoke upward. Next you can lower the censer and say, "Here I mark the boundary of that which is below."

For your review, here is a brief outline of creating a ritual circle:

1. Prepare your altar setup

2. Mark out the ritual circle area with a rope, stones, votive candles,or other objects

3. Activate the altar by calling upon the elemental forces

4. Cast the ritual circle with the ritual tools

5. Evoke and invoke the quarter guardians

6. Affirm the sphere of the ritual circle

7. Declare the work completed in the names of your Goddess and God

Now that we have looked at the process of establishing a ritual circle, let us turn now to an examination of the components of ritual techniques and structure.

There are essentially five components that comprise the art of creating successful rituals. You can adapt them or arrange them according to your own needs, but I strongly recommend that you incorporate them all into your ritual design. They are as follows:

1. Personal Will

2. Timing

3. Imagery

4. Direction

5. Balance

Let's look at each one separately.

THE WILL: This can also be thought of as motivation, temptation, or persuasion. You must be sufficiently motivated to perform a ritual or work of magic in order to establish enough power to accomplish your goal. If you care little about the results, or put only a small amount of energy into your desire, then you are unlikely to see any real results. The stronger the need or desire, the more likely it is that you will raise the amount of energy required to bring about the change you seek. But desire or need is not enough by itself.

TIMING: In the performance of ritual magic, timing can mean success or failure. The best time to cast a spell or create a work of magic is when the target is most receptive. Receptivity is usually assured when the target is passive. Therefore, choose a time when the target of your intent is not active but is passive and therefore receptive. Take into account the phase of the moon, which should be waxing for gainful intentions and waning for dissolving intentions. In essence, you want to work with Nature and not against it. Generally speaking, 4:00 AM in the target zone area is the most effective time to cast a spell of influence because this is generally a passive and receptive time in our society

IMAGERY: The success of any work also depends upon images created by the mind. This is where the imagery enters into the formula. Anything that serves to intensify the emotions will help generate images with vitality, and therefore add to the successful outcome of the ritual's design. Any drawing, statue, photo, scent, article of clothing, sound, or situation that helps you to merge with your desire will greatly contribute to your success. Imagery is a constant reminder of what you wish to attract or accomplish. It serves as a homing device in its role as a representation of the object, person, or situation that is your target or ritual intention. Imagery can be shaped and directed according to the will of your mind. This becomes the pattern or formula that leads to the realization of desire. Surround yourself with images of your desire, and the vibrations will resonate and magnetically attract your intention.

DIRECTION: Once enough energy has been raised, you must direct it toward your desire. Do not be anxious concerning the results because anxiety will act to draw the energy back to you before it can take effect. Reflecting back upon the spell tends to ground the energy because it draws the images and concepts back to you. Try to give the matter no more thought so as not to deplete its effectiveness. After your ritual, mark a seven-day period on your calendar and evaluate the results at the end of this period. It usually takes about seven days for magic to manifest (one lunar quarter).

BALANCE: The last aspect of magic to take into account is personal balance. This means that one must consider the need for the work of magic and the consequences upon both the spell caster and the target. If anger motivates your magical work, then wait a few hours or sleep on it overnight. While anger can be a useful propellant for a ritual intent, it can also cloud the thinking and therefore be detrimental to you. If possible, make sure you have exhausted the normal means of dealing with something before you move to a magical solution. Make sure you are feeling well enough to work magic, and plan to rest afterward. Magic requires a portion of your vital living essence, which is drawn from your aura and body energy centers. Replenish this with rest even if you do not feel tired. Health problems begin in the aura long before the body is aware of them.

Having looked at the mechanics of ritual, it is time now to consider the nature and the roles of the ritual tools in your tradition. There are two different schools of thought related to the tools, and we should consider them both. The primary differences center on the assignment of the elemental forces to specific tools. This applies specifically to the wand and the athame, but a general review of each tool will help you decide how you wish to organize all of this within your tradition.

THE PENTACLE: Traditionally, a tool assigned the element of earth. As such it is most appropriately constructed from clay or some metal mined from rock. Bronze, brass, or iron are very common substances for a pentacle. Ceramic pentacles are also popular. The pentacle is perhaps the least mystical of the four tools and is therefore often used in relatively mundane context. Many traditions use it as a platter upon which to place and bless or consecrate ritual objects.

On a magical level, the pentacle can be used to ground or stabilize energy, as well as for protection in the form of a shield. As such, it can be placed to temporarily seal a breach in the circle (as in the case of opening a doorway to the outside). It can also be used to protect against unwanted energy directed toward your ritual setting. Unruly spirits can also be shielded against by holding the pentacle out toward them within the circle. The design of the pentagram on the pentacle's surface is very effective for such uses.

On a spiritual level, the pentacle represents valor and bravery. In this light, it is the shield of the spiritual warrior. On an occult level, the pentacle is assigned to the material body of the ritualist.

THE WAND: The wand has two different elemental assignments, and so you will want to select one that works best for you. One elemental assignment is fire and the other is air. For simplicity, I will deal here with the assignment of air. For the assignment of fire, see the section on the athame, and simply make the switch of representations.

The wand is traditionally made of wood, and among the oldest references we find mention of the oak, willow, and beech. Air represents the mind and mental communication. When assigned to the wand, air is a gentle but powerful force. The wand is compelling in contrast to the athame, for example, which is exacting by comparison. It is for this reason that deity is called with a wand rather than an athame. Spirit allies are also called with the use of the wand. One exception is the guardians, which are traditionally summoned with the athame.

The wand is also used to direct blessings and to bestow them. In initiation ceremonies, the wand is used to bless the initiate by touching various areas of the body. In lunar rites, the wand is used to draw down the moon upon the high priestess.

On a spiritual level, the wand represents intuition and foresight. In this light, it is the far-reaching lance of the spiritual warrior. On an occult level, the wand is assigned to the mental intention of the ritualist.

THE ATHAME: Like the wand, the athame has two different elemental assignments. One is fire and the other is air. For the purposes of this section, I will deal with the athame as a tool of elemental fire. If you prefer the air assignment, then use the alignments in the wand section.

As a tool of fire, the athame represents raw energy or force, the element in which the metal blade was forged. It is a tool of the emotions as opposed to a tool of the mind (the latter being the nature of the wand). The athame is traditionally used to cast a ritual circle, and through its actions a protective sphere of elemental fire is established. Fire is the force of transformation and is required to change ordinary mundane reality into a mystical event.

In some traditions, the athame is used to challenge new initiates seeking initiation. The blade is typically pressed against the chest and the initiate is admonished not to continue unless he or she is prepared to fully accept what lies ahead. The athame is also used to banish unwanted spirits and entities from the ritual setting.

On a spiritual level, the athame represents controlled and directed emotions. In this light, it is a sword of the spiritual warrior. On an occult level, the athame is assigned to the emotional energy of the ritualist.

THE CHALICE: Traditionally, the chalice is made of silver and serves to contain the ritual wine. Like the pentacle, the chalice serves a more practical nature in a ritual setting. However, because it contains the sacred wine and is a vessel through which spiritual nourishment is provided, the chalice cannot be assigned to the mundane. It is featured in the rite of Cakes and Wine.

In essence, the chalice symbolizes receptivity and, like the cauldron, it is a womb symbol intimately connected to the Goddess. Its mate is the wand, a tool intimately linked to the God. Together they combine to enact the Great Rite, which is the divine union of Goddess and God nature.

On a spiritual level, the chalice represents compassion and acceptance. In this light, it is the heart of the spiritual warrior. On an occult level, the chalice is assigned to the spiritual awareness of the ritualist.

The Four Elements in Ritual and Magic

An integral part of any ritual or work of magic is inclusion of the four elements. These vital forces are the building blocks of creation and manifestation. When incorporating them into a ritual, it is helpful to understand their natures and how they influence the energy and intent of the ritual's design. Let's break each one down into very simple understandings:

1. Earth: The quality of this element is to stabilize, to strengthen, and to give foundation. It is used to encourage manifestation and to balance the element of water, which is formless. It is also used to reduce the overactivity of the element of fire, and to slow the abundance of the element of air. The evocational/invocational tonal of earth is the vowel sound of the letter A, elongated into a deep tonal chant: AAAAAAAAAAAAAAAAAAAAAAAA.

2. Air: The quality of this element is to transmit, to convey, and to communicate. It is used to carry images, scents, and sounds in an astral manner. It is also used to stimulate earth and water, and to revitalize fire. The evocational/invocational tonal of air is the vowel sound of the letter E, elongated into a deep tonal chant: EEEEEEEEEEEEEEEEEEEEEE.

3. Fire: The quality of this element is to energize, radiate, and transform. It is used to alter forms, whether material or astral. It is also used to stimulate or diminish inactive water (as in boiling), reduce overabundance of air, and change the composition of earth. Fire is the preferred element by which to cast circles because of its transformational properties and its natural quality as a barrier. The evocational/invocational tonal of fire is the vowel sound of the letter I, elongated into a deep tonal chant: IIIIIIIIIIIIIIIIIIIIIIII IIIIIIII.

4. Water: The quality of this element is movement, liquefaction, and purification. It is used to create motion and adaptability, and to dissolve substances. It is also used to diminish the overactivity of fire, to alter the solidity of earth, and to slow the activity of air. The evocational/invocational tonal of water is the vowel sound of the letter O, elongated into a deep tonal chant: OOOOOOOOOOOOOOOOOO.

In circle casting, the tonals for each element can be sounded at each quarter to evoke the presence of each corresponding elemental nature. While the circle is being cast with the athame, the tonal of fire can be chanted. This is particularly effective when the coven members chant the tonal as someone casts the circle. This person can join in and/or recite the words for evoking the circle, which are prescribed by the tradition.

Ritual Signs and Gestures

There are a variety of signs and gestures to choose from when designing your tradition. These become a form of communication within a tradition. The use of signs and gestures can enhance the ritual experience and can draw upon Otherworld energies. These are presented in the chapter on the book of shadows.

Wiccan Symbols

There are various symbols that can be incorporated into your tradition. They can be used to mark sacred objects, enhance the texts of your tradition, or keep things secret that you do not wish prying eyes to discover. A variety of symbols are depicted in the chapter on the book of shadows.

Now that we have explored the components and themes associated with constructing rituals, let's turn to the next chapter and examine the application of ritual patterns.

six

RITUAL PATTERNS

Rituals within a religious system commonly contain elements of the theology of the tradition. In modern Wicca, we find these themes appearing as reflections of the mythos as it relates to the Goddess and God. Wicca incorporates the Wheel of the Year story into its rituals as well as other secondary themes of a religious or mystical nature. The latter includes such figures as the Oak King and Holly King, the Green Man, and the Harvest Lord.

In this chapter, we will examine the religious, magical, and mystical natures of the figures that appear in Wiccan rites. We will also look at examples of ritual format. In this way, you may consider how you want to incorporate these vital aspects of Wiccan theology and ritual format. Let's begin with a review of the secondary figures in Wiccan legend and lore.

In the tale of the Oak and Holly King figures, we find two brothers who compete for reign over the waxing and waning seasons of the year. As we noted earlier, the Oak King rules from the Winter Solstice through to the Summer Solstice, and the position is reversed for the Holly King. In the general mythos of the two kings, we find them also competing for the favor of the White Goddess. The figures appear to be connected to others known as the Oak Knight and Holly Knight, and the Winter

King and Summer King, who can all be found in old lore. Their appearance is brief, their legends vague and obscure, but despite this, they persist in Wicca through their connection with the solstice periods. The importance of the Oak King and Holly King is that we can use their images and meanings to mark the waxing and waning periods and to keep pace with them in our own lives. This helps to keep us in balance, both internally and externally, with the forces of Nature.

The Green Man is a figure who, not unlike the Oak and Holly Kings, is associated with the seasons though plant life. Although the history of the Green Man is unclear and widely debated, in modern Wicca he is the personification of the plant kingdom. In this light, we can also associate or equate him with the Woodland Lord, also known as the hooded one. In essence, the Green Man represents the tenacity of the life force itself. This theme is also reflected in the Harvest Lord. The importance of the Green Man is that his imagery serves as an umbilical cord to the vitality of Nature. By using his imagery, we can maintain a healthy flow of nature's energy into our lives.

The Harvest Lord is an old figure that also appears in folklore and folk ballads such as John Barleycorn. Like the Green Man, he is associated with the plant kingdom. However, the Harvest Lord is specifically connected to cultivated crops, unlike the Green Man, who is the spirit of the wild woods. In Wiccan lore, the Harvest Lord represents the cycles of life from seed to sheaf and back again. The importance of the Harvest Lord is that his imagery, and the meanings expressed within, unite the pattern of our lives to the promise of renewed life.

The Harvest Lord is a type of Slain God figure, the willing sacrifice, the sacred king and sacred seed. He is cut down and his seeds planted into the earth so that life may continue and be ever more abundant. This mythos is symbolic of the planted seed nourished beneath the soil and the ascending sprout that becomes the harvested plant by the time of the Autumn Equinox.

This mystical theme of transformation associated with agriculture is found in many European folk tales. The mythos of the Harvest Lord is preserved in ancient texts dating from Homer and Hesiod, and up into modern folklore. It is perhaps best preserved in the story of the passion of the flax and the dying god. In ancient Greece, he was *Linos*, in Lithuania he was *Vaizgantas,* and in Scotland he was known as *Barleycorn.*

It is interesting to note that the common word for flax in European language unites Old Europe with Celtic Europe. In Greek it is *linon*, in Latin *linum*, and the Old Irish is *lin*, which is also true of Old German. This general mythos is also reflected in the Hans Christian Andersen story of the flax, and in the Danish tale of Rye's Pain (Rugen's Pine).

Essentially, such tales address the planting of the seed and its struggle to sprout from the earth. This is followed by it having to endure the elements. Then, in its prime, the flax is pulled out of the ground and subjected to thrashing, soaking, and roasting. Eventually it is combed with hackle-combs and thorns, spun into thread, and woven into linen. Finally it is cut and pierced with needles and sown into a shirt. In all of this, we find the theme of the sacrifice of the Harvest Lord for the welfare of his people.

In the classical Greek myth of the god Dionysos, he is first slain and then dismembered. Next he is boiled, roasted, and then devoured. The Orphic myth of Dionysos includes the same sequence but adds the recomposition and resurrection of the bones. Ancient writers such as Heraclitus remark that Dionysos and Hades are one and the same, thus associating Dionysos with the Underworld (a classic Wiccan mythos, the Lord of the Shadows). Further evidence of this connection comes from the labyrinth tale of the Minotaur, Dionysos, and Ariadne. The labyrinth symbolized the Underworld, and Ariadne (mistress of the labyrinth) symbolized the funerary goddess. The marriage of Dionysos and Ariadne, celebrated during the Anthesteria (an ancient springtime festival), coincided with the periodic return to the earth of the souls of the dead. This is of particular importance because it connects Dionysos with the souls of the dead and the Underworld.

The essential theme of the Slain God concept is rooted in the notion of the early hunter/warrior cults that existed prior to the formation of agrarian societies. In the early tribal states, hunters and warriors held a prominent place in the social structure. The bravest and most cunning hunter/warrior was honored within the tribe and was looked upon as a leader. The well-being of this individual affected the well-being of the tribe. This is a theme that we find in the King Arthur mythos of northern Europe, where the land and the king are one. It is also reflected in the southern European mythos of Rex Nemorensis, King of the Woods in the sacred grove of Diana of Lake Nemi.

Before the invention of farming and herding, the hunt was essential to the preservation of life. Without successful hunters, the tribes would perish. Hunting was dangerous because early primitive weapons required that the hunters be close to their prey. Bodily injuries were common, and many hunters lost their lives or became lame as a result of the hunt. The hunter was also the tribal warrior, risking his life for the sake of his people. The needs of the tribe, whether for food or defense, required sending out the best the tribe could offer.

This concept evolved along with the evolution of religious and spiritual consciousness. The concept of deity and its role in life and death took shape within ritual and dogma. The idea arose of sending the best member of the tribe directly to the gods to secure the needs of the tribe. This was the birth of human sacrifice, and those who went willingly were believed to become gods themselves.

Offerings were nothing new to our ancient ancestors; many times food and flowers or game were laid out before the gods. To offer one of your own was considered the highest offering the tribe could make. Among human offerings, the sacrifice of a willing individual was the greatest gift the tribe could offer; the gods would surely grant the tribe anything if someone willingly gave his or her life to them.

The blood and flesh of the sacrifice were distributed among the clan and given into the soil. Parts of the body were buried in cultivated fields to ensure the harvest. Small portions of the body and blood were added to the ceremonial feast. This ancient practice was later symbolically incorporated into Christianity in the rite of Communion as the body and blood of the Christ figure.

In the Slain God mythos, sacrifice is only part of the story. The sacrificial offering must be returned to the tribe. To accomplish this, rituals were designed to resurrect the Slain God. Special maidens were prepared to bring about the birth, usually virgins who were artificially inseminated so that no human male could be pointed to as the father. Bloodlines were carefully traced from the impregnated female, and the returning soul was looked for among her children.

As human consciousness matured and evolved, human sacrifice was replaced entirely by animal sacrifice. Animal sacrifice was later replaced by plant sacrifice, the harvest festival. The same ancient mythos applied to both animal and plant sacrifice. In the Wiccan mystery tradition, we find the theme of the "eating of deity" or consuming of the Harvest Lord in the ritual cakes and wine (flesh and blood) ritual.

In the ancient tradition, it was through the connection of the body and blood of the Slain God that the people became one with deity. This is essentially the concept of the Christian rite of Communion or Eucharistic Celebration. At the "Last Supper," Jesus declares to his followers that the bread and wine are his body. He then declares that he will lay down his life for his people, and bids them to eat of his flesh and drink of his blood (the bread and the wine). Blood was believed to contain the essence of the life force. The death of the king freed the sacred inner spirit. By distributing his flesh and blood, heaven and earth were united and his vital energy renewed the kingdom.

The Slain God appears in various aspects throughout the ages. His image can be seen in Jack-in-the-Green, the Hooded Man, the Green Man, and the Hanged Man of the Tarot. He is the Lord of Vegetation, the harvest, and in his free untamed aspect he is the forest. In the Green Man image, the Slain God is the spirit of the land manifesting in all plant forms. He is the procreative power and the seed of life.

The Slain God is, in effect, a bridge between the worlds. This is why he is often depicted as either tied to, or hung from, a tree. The tree bridges the gap between the Underworld and the Heavens, for it is rooted in the earth and its branches reach into the sky. The Slain God is one with heaven and earth, and to be one with him is to be one with the Source of All Things.

Ritual Formats

Each of the Sabbat rituals is constructed around the celebration of a particular season and the veneration of the deities associated with the corresponding time of year. Incorporated into each Sabbat is a portion or reflection of the myths that are connected to the deities. This serves to unite all elements together and through this to establish the necessary alignments for the ritual celebrants.

The format for each Sabbat is also intended to bring the celebrants into an awareness of their life stages, which are symbolized by the myths of the deities and the general theme of the season. The ideas of planting, nurturing, harvesting, and preserving are all metaphors for the endurance of human life. Even though most Wiccans are not farmers, the seasonal themes still speak to family, career, lifetime goals, and the preparation for old age.

Woven into the structure of Wiccan rites is the principle of giving something back in exchange for what is received. This is reflected in the placing of offerings to the deities and the requests for aid or favor. Through this, we acknowledge that all things are connected and are in relationship with one another.

Fertility is the underlying principle in the seasonal rites of Wicca. This is not only a means of returning fertility to the earth so that we replenish what we have drawn, but is also about the fruitfulness of our lives. This relates to all facets including children, career, creativity, prosperity, and health.

In the winter, we ask what can bring renewal to our lives? What in our lives calls for rebirth in our relationships, work, goals, and dreams? What plans do we need to make in order to bring renewal and rebirth into our lives? What is our Child of Promise?

When spring arrives, we ask what are the symbolic seeds we need to plant in order to achieve our desired harvest? What symbolic weeds have spoiled the garden of our relationships, career, goals, and dreams? What actions can we take to remove these weeds and clear our garden? When is the best time to prepare and plant the garden?

In summer, we ask what have we achieved in our lives that we feel good about? What is good about us as the individuals we have become? In what area of our lives is there abundance and prosperity? In what area of our lives is there growth?

With the arrival of fall, we ask what in our lives no longer serves us or others? What do we need to shed or rid ourselves of? What in our lives taps our energy and drains us? What can we do without? What must be cut away that will allow needed and new growth in our lives for the future? What seeds do we retain for a new season of life to come? These are the things that Wiccan rites can lead us to embrace in mind, body, and spirit.

When we break down the groupings of Wiccan rites, we note that the eight Sabbats fall into groups of two sets of four rituals, one in the waxing half of the year, and the other in the waning. The four rituals of each half alternate between an evening celebration and a daytime festival.

The Winter Solstice, or Yule, reflects the idea of the sun as a divine image. The essential theme of the Winter Solstice is focused upon renewal and rebirth. Here we find the metaphor of the survival and return of the light, which we can liken to the journey of the soul from lifetime to lifetime. In a religious sense, the Winter Solstice is the promise of the undying soul. It is also the covenant between the divine source and the spark that we call the soul. This covenant marks the promise that we shall never be abandoned by the source from which we were created.

In the mystery tradition, the Winter Solstice is celebrated as the birth of the Sun God, the Child of Promise for the coming year of new light. Our ancestors created a mythos that began with birth because it is the natural act of entry into the material world. In this core concept, we find the connections of fertility and a Mother Goddess, which is the foundation of the ways contained in Wiccan religion.

The ancient veneration of a tree as a dwelling place for a god also appears in the figure of the Yule tree. The tree, as a Yule log, has long been associated with the Winter Solstice. In some traditions the Yule log is burned, and in other traditions a lighted candle is set upon it. In ancient times, fire had to be drawn, or *birthed,* from wood. This involved using a wooden drill to create friction. In effect, this wooden rod or shaft penetrated the log, and from this act a flame was generated. Here we can see the log giving birth to the flame, which is the divine light.

The traditions associated with the Yule season, even in modern times, are rooted in Pagan concepts and imagery. When we picture a hearth, stockings hung upon it, and a fire burning within it, we are looking at the ancient grotto of the Goddess. The woven stockings are symbols of the Fates who weave the patterns of life and death. The log and the fire are mated pairs, aspects of the divine source that manifest as masculine and feminine polarities.

It is easy to confuse the concepts related to fire regarding which gender is assigned to its manifestation. In the earliest writings in Western literature, fire is the goddess Hestia, later known to the Romans as Vesta. This can cause us to view fire as specifically feminine. However, if we consider that all things issue forth from the Mother Goddess, then it is easy to reconcile a flame (generated from the Goddess) as the masculine part of the feminine whole.

We know from ancient times that fire was believed to dwell within wood. This belief arose from the fact that fire could seemingly be drawn out of the wood by a rapid rubbing action. In later times, a glass lens was used (in the same way a magnifying glass is used to burn wood by focusing sunlight). An ancient custom required fire to be drawn from a piece of the sacred tree of a grove sanctuary, and for the flame to be passed to a torch. The torch was used to carry the divine fire to the new grove where it was then ritually / magically passed into the new sanctuary.

In the mythos of the mystery tradition, the Sun God is the guardian of the sacred coven. What he protects is the divine source, focused in the sacred tree, which is the Great Goddess. In this aspect, he appears as the Stag-Horned God, Lord of the Woods. However, the focal point of the Winter Solstice is not upon this older form of the Sun God, but instead focuses upon his birth as the Child of Promise, who brings new light. This light serves to renew the material and spiritual essence within and without. The Child of Promise is the seed of new hope, renewal, and new growth.

The festival of Imbolc celebrates the coming of spring and the release of the winter's hold upon the land. In Celtic lands, the festival marked what has come to be called the Day of Bride, another name for the goddess Brighid (also known as Brigit). One old legend features Bride as a captive in the realm of winter, where she is held for three days. She escapes and emerges at Imbolc as a youthful maiden, after drinking from the Well of Youth. Here we find the theme of transformation associated with Imbolc.

In another legend associated with Bride, she bears a magical wand. One touch of her wand turns the land green, and brings forth the white and yellow flowers of spring. The wand is symbolic of the fertilizing and impregnating forces over which the Goddess has power. This metaphysical aspect is reflected in the mundane world where the sexuality of women can influence the behavior of men, who are the fertilizing and impregnating vessels. The power of women over men, and the power of the Goddess over the fertilizing forces of Nature are reflections of the same essence.

In Scotland, an old folk custom featured sculpting a bundled sheaf of grain into the image of a woman. This image symbolized the youthful and pure maiden, who would later become the May Queen. The sheaf was typically saved from the last harvest before the winter season that preceded Imbolc. Here we find the connection between the Earth Mother and the Harvest Lord, for it is into the womb/body of the Goddess that the slain Harvest Lord returns. He is reborn, and later dies as the Straw Man, the harvested sheaf that represents the Sun God.

In the mystery tradition, at the time of Imbolc, the Goddess is called the Lady of Fire and the God is the Lord of Ice. Folk traditions associate a female figure wearing a crown of candles with the Imbolc season. Here we see the Goddess of Fire as the reigning queen. It is she who raises the passion and inflames the energy of the God (note the symbolism of Bride's wand). The God has been bound in the Underworld since he entered there as the Harvest Lord. The ice represents the stillness of the Underworld water on which the God lays in his reed basket boat. The passion of the God is awakened by the flame desire of the Goddess, which frees him from being bound and allows the Underworld river to flow back into the world of the living. Water is an important element in the Spring season (Equinox) where we find the Goddess as the Lady of the Lake, and the God as the Lord of the Reeds.

The Spring Equinox marks the renewal of the life force within the land. The seeds that have slept beneath the blanket of winter now begin to feel the quickening of energy. In the mystery tradition, we find the tale of the Goddess ascending from the Underworld (like the moon rising from beneath the horizon). The God rises also and follows her in a ritual of courtship. Here we find myths attached to the cycles of the sun following the moon and the moon following the sun through the sky.

Fertility was the essence of the season, and ancient rites were centered on the theme of fertility. The plowing of furrows and the planting of seeds held sexual symbolism. The theme of ripening sexuality associated the adolescent phase of life with the preparation of the coming growing season and the eventual time of harvest. This was expressed in myth as a young maiden goddess and a young lord.

With the melting of winter ice as the weather grew warmer, water appeared in the lakes and wetlands. Lakes have long been associated with the Underworld and the Otherworld. Ancient beliefs held that lakes were gateways leading down into these other realms. The ancient mystical figure known as the Lady of the Lake is rooted in this old belief.

Around the lakes and in the wetlands, reeds grew quickly. These reeds were used to make harvest baskets, and such baskets appear as cradles in the birth myths of various sun gods. One example is that of the god Dionysos (the divine child born on the Winter Solstice), who is set adrift in a harvest basket. Another example appears in the tale of Llew, who is cast adrift by his mother, who places him in a basket made of weed and sedge. Here we find that water and the seed within the harvest basket join together, uniting the cycles of life and death.

The Goddess, as a maiden figure at spring, represents the new fertile season (just as the developing body of the adolescent female signals her coming into womanhood). The God, as the young woodland lord in spring, symbolizes the mating drive. The maiden quickens his energy with her allure, and fertility awakens in the plant and animal kingdoms.

The festival of Beltane celebrates the renewal of life as the forces of spring begin to manifest the buds and flowers and greenery of Nature. The Goddess now appears on the earth in her aspect of the young maiden. The God appears as a young male in his prime phase of fertility. It is here in this season that the courtship begins, which will lead to abundant crops and herds as the blessings of the union of Goddess and God spread throughout all of Nature.

In ancient times, bonfires were lighted on hilltops in a custom based on a belief that the light of the fire attracted the sun. Following a long, cold winter, such an act held great importance. Beltane also included fertility rites, which included lovemaking in the freshly plowed furrows of the planting fields. Customs included the crowning of a May Queen and May King, who oversaw games of competition and reward. Folkloric figures such as the hobbyhorse and Green Man were featured during the festival of Beltane.

In northern Europe, among the first trees to blossom near Beltane is the hawthorn. The hawthorn has a long association with the Elven/Faery race. In ancient legend, the hawthorn is a guardian tree that protects the entrance to magical realms. One ancient belief held that an oak and ash tree flanked the pillars to portals that opened to the faery realm. The hawthorn tree guarded access to the oak and ash portal. In this sense, the hawthorn became a symbol of initiation and passage, as well as guardianship.

As we have previously seen, the tree is a gateway and bridge between the realms that we call the Overworld, Middleworld, and Underworld. One May Day custom involved gathering bundles of wood from the field and forest. These branches were separated and tied together into small bundles, then hung over doorways to protect the household. A long pole called the Maypole was decorated with ribbons and placed in the center of the town or village. Dancers would hold the ends of the ribbons and intertwine them in a crisscross and weaving dance that led them inward toward the pole.

The Maypole represented, among other things, the phallus of fertility that impregnates all of Nature. The colored ribbons were intended to revitalize the fertile essence by binding renewal to the Maypole phallus. Customs varied throughout Europe as to the colors involved. The most common colors were white (renewal of the bone with new life), and red (the vital blood of life). Other colors included green, blue, yellow, and additional hues associated with love and spring.

Various folk magic customs are connected to the Maypole dance. One of the primary customs involved men and women forming an alternating circle around the Maypole. Traditionally, the men take the white ribbons and the women take the red. The men turn to face their left and take one step out from the pole. This creates two circles of dancers facing one another. The music begins and the dancers start a weaving dance, moving their ribbon over the first person they meet and under the next. The dance continues, over and under, until the wound ribbons are too short for the dance to continue. The men and women then embrace and begin the celebration.

The Summer Solstice marks the celebration of growth and the fertility of Nature. In the Aegean/Mediterranean regions, fireflies swarm and mate at this time. In folklore, the glowing light of the firefly at night connected Midsummer's Eve to the faery legends. The yellow blossom of St. John's Wort resembled the color of the firefly. Therefore the herb was believed to possess magical powers when harvested on the morning of the Summer Solstice.

In many European traditions, this season is intimately linked to faery lore. The popular play *A Midsummer Night's Dream* is rooted in such lore. In ancient times, it was believed that faeries brought about the flowers, fruits, and the general abundance of Nature. Therefore, Summer was the peak of their power and a time of celebration and revelry.

In the mystery tradition, the Summer Solstice also marked the wedding of the Goddess and God. Here they reigned as the Lord of the Plant and Animal Kingdom, and the Queen of Nature. Because the Summer Solstice is the longest day of the year, the God was considered to be at the height of his prowess. His power and vitality radiates into the land, and before his strength fails he must be taken in his prime.

There is an ancient theme that the well-being of the king and the well-being of the land (and the Kingdom) are tied together. In this mythos, whatever becomes of the king then befalls the land and the people. At the core of this mythos is the theme of the Sacrificial King, who is also known as the Slain God figure. These figures are part of the character known as the Harvest Lord. Summer marks the beginning of the harvest season, which concludes with the onset of Autumn.

The festival of Lughnasadh celebrates the beginning of the harvest season in northern Europe. It is technically the gathering of the first fruits of Nature's bounty. It is here that the mythos turns to the theme of the whole and the parts. An ancient concept held that the earth was the mother, which made seed crops the son of the mother. Since it is the seed that impregnates the earth (from an ancient perspective) the seed is both the lover and the son of the Great Mother. In this sense, the season of Lughnasadh reflects the separation of mother and child so that the expansion of life may continue.

In the mystery tradition, the season known in modern times as Lughnasadh finds the Goddess as the Lady of the Fields, and the God is seen as the Lord of the Barley. This demonstrates the relationship between the two deity forms, with the Goddess as the fertile field and the God as the ripened grain that issues forth from within her. Here we clearly see the whole and the parts of the whole manifest within Nature.

In northern Europe, the time of Lughnasadh was a popular one for handfasting ceremonies (marriages). This may have been related to the seasonal theme of the separation of parent and child, and so the couple joins together as independent from parental reign. This season was also favored for the observation of omens, which is rooted in the awakening of the Underworld forces during the act of harvesting the planted fields. The Underworld forces have long been considered vital to foretelling the future.

As a ritual celebration, Lughnasadh is the time of anticipation of plenty, reflected in the abundant crops in the cultivated fields at this season. This is the offspring of the Goddess, the fruit of her womb issued forth from the rich, fertile soil. Within the bounty of Nature the god seed is contained in the grain, fruit, and vegetables, which will ensure the future harvest crops of yet another season to come.

The Autumn Equinox marks the period of the final harvesting, the time of the last gathering-in. This is the season of celebrating the bounty of Nature. Here the Earth Mother has given birth to all the fruits of the earth. Therein reside the seeds of her son, the Lord of the Harvest.

In a Wiccan mythos, we find a tale assigning the spirit of the land to the Harvest Lord figure. In this belief, the spirit of the land is drawn into the sheaves of grain as they are cut and gathered. Here the Harvest Lord leaps from bale to bale as the threshers harvest the field. When the last sheaf is gathered and bound, the Lord of the Harvest remains fixed to the field. In a time-honored ritual, the spirit of the land is then returned to the earth.

The Autumn Equinox also marks the beginning of the descent of the Goddess into the Underworld. In this mythos, she journeys to find and retrieve her lost lover. This is a metaphor for the harvested fields that now lay void of the summer's abundance. The gathered seeds of the Sun God are now stored away, and the renewal of life is asleep within the spirit of the land.

The season of Samhain marks the parting of the fabric that separates the world of the living from the Otherworld realm. Here we find the Goddess in her aspect as the Lady of Shadow, and the God as the Lord of Shadow. In a related mythos, they are viewed as the King and Queen of the Faery Kingdom, and as the Lord and Lady of the Underworld who oversee the ancestral realm. This relates to an ancient belief in the spirits of the dead and the use of primitive burial mounds. In time such mounds became connected with faery hills in folklore and folk magic.

In the mystery tradition, the Otherworld/Underworld is intimately associated with the ancestral spirit. This is imagined as a collective consciousness that contains and preserves the memories of all who came before us. In the Italian system, this is depicted as an entity known as the *Lare*. In the mystery tradition, the skull represents what remains after death, the memory and experience of those who once lived in the material world. It is honored as a guardian, preserver, and escort who stands at the threshold between this world and the next.

The well-known image of the skull and crossbones appears in the oldest forms of the mysteries. The crossed bones symbolize guardianship over the gateway into the Otherworld. The skull represents ancestral knowledge, wisdom, and oracle power. In the mystery tradition, a candle is placed on top of the skull, and when lighted, it symbolizes communication between the worlds.

It was an ancient belief that blood vitalized the spirits of the dead and granted them the ability to speak to the living. Therefore, a few drops of blood were offered to the ancestral spirits in order to establish direct and reliable communication. In modern Wiccan mysteries, this is often symbolized by placing a red candle on the skull. Red represents blood and vitality, and is therefore a symbol of the living ancestral spirit.

The old tradition of bobbing for apples at Halloween is rooted in the mysteries of this ancient seasonal celebration. The apple has long been associated with the faery realm, and in ancient legend it served as food for those who journeyed into the Otherworld. Since legend held that eating any food in the faery realm prohibited anyone from leaving, the taking of apples into the faery realm allowed one to eat and still return. Water was intimately connected to the Otherworld/Underworld, and sacred lakes and wells were often considered to be entrances into the hidden realms. In this view, bobbing for apples symbolizes the initiatory journey into the Otherworld/Underworld and the ability to return again through eating the sacred fruit.

Many ancient legends in northern Europe speak of the silver bough that allowed mortals safe passage to and from the faery realm. The bough was said to bear apples (usually nine in number) that were sacred to the Faery Queen, who granted protection to all who bore the sacred bough. In southern Europe, the golden bough served much the same purpose, and appears in the tale of Aeneas who is guided into the Underworld by a Sybil who helps secures the golden bough for him to bear on his journey.

Now that we have completed looking at ritual formats and at the inner mystery themes within them, you can better understand the various levels within the Sabbat rituals (and how they function together). In the appendices section you will find examples of each of the eight Sabbat rites for group practice (175–208) or for solitary rites (209–230). These rituals are based upon the mystery tradition rites and can be easily modified for other types of Wiccan ritual themes. Use them as templates or ideas for creating your own rites. The signs, postures, and gestures mentioned in these rituals can be found in the chapter on the book of shadows.

Add coven songs and chants to the rites where you feel they are appropriate. It is beneficial to fill parts of the ritual with song or chant whenever coven members are waiting for whatever reason. This helps to keep life within the ritual. Remember that all these rituals are templates and it is expected that people will bring their intuition and spontaneity to the otherwise structured rituals.

seven

INITIATION AND METAPHYSICAL
ASPECTS OF WICCA

The topic of initiation may well be the most controversial topic in modern Wicca. There are those who even question its place in the tradition to begin with. Be that as it may, there are two basic types of initiation that we encounter in Wicca. One is a simple, light-hearted welcoming rite similar to joining a mundane club or organization. The other type is formalized ritual, serious in nature, and performed by individuals who were initiated by others in a chain of experienced initiators and teachers.

In modern Wicca, we also find two other types of ceremony. One is the rite of dedication, in which a person formally declares his or her intention to study Wicca for a year and day. The other type of ceremony is called self-initiation, which is the notion that a person can initiate herself or himself. But before we examine the different types of initiation, it can be helpful to consider the meaning of the word itself.

The English word "initiation" comes from the Latin *initiare*, which itself is derived from the Latin *initium*. The basic meaning is "to begin or to be admitted into something as a member." In the literal meaning of the word, the act is little more than a formality. However, in a mystical or occult sense, initiation is something more complex. We will examine this later in the chapter, but for now let's look at the basic forms related to initiation into Wicca.

Dedication

The purpose of the dedication period is for the person to study and explore Wicca in order to decide if this is their religion of choice. The traditional period of time is a year and day, which is a theme commonly found in old Celtic tales of mystical journey. During this time, the seeker commits to study and instruction. Typically this involves an assignment of reading material and training exercises. The goal is to familiarize the seeker with the core elements of the tradition and to provide various indications of what it's like to live life as a Wiccan.

In modern Wicca, this can be a personal commitment to oneself, or it can be a formal contract between student and teacher. The period exists in order to allow enough time to understand the path of Wicca and to work out any concerns or personal issues. One of the primary challenges many people face is to break through the erroneous stereotypes about paths like Wicca in Judeo Christian-dominated Western culture.

When considering joining a group or coven, it is not uncommon for the seeker to be asked to discuss past events, issues, or training that may present challenges to embracing Wicca as a spiritual or religious path. In this regard, think about issues such as ritual nudity, intimacy, and other things that you may or may not want to include in your tradition. If you do, then it is wise to have a long heart-to-heart discussion with any seeker during the dedication stage. You may want to create a questionnaire similar to a job application, but customized to address various feelings and past experiences. Knowing if in the past someone was abused, raped, or in prison is important information for group dynamics. This can help you avoid very unpleasant events in the future.

When the seeker is ready to commit to a dedication, then a simple rite is beneficial. It can include the lighting of a candle and some incense in a quiet setting. The seeker can anoint himself or herself with a pleasant oil fragrance, and then speak words to this effect:

> *I hereby dedicate myself to a period of one year and day, during which time I will commit to a serious and thoughtful study of Wicca. I will approach this with an open mind and open heart. By the honor of my word I do so swear to undertake and complete this journey of dedication.*

There is one last word of advice I have to offer regarding this commitment: Make sure that you and the seeker have the same understanding of what it means to give one's word or to swear an oath. I have unfortunately discovered in the past that to some people a sworn oath holds only while it is convenient. You will want to avoid discovering this too late and having therefore wasted much of your time, energy, and trust.

Initiation

Once a decision has been made to practice Wicca, a rite of initiation traditionally follows. Typically, this is performed on the night of a new moon or full moon. As previously mentioned, in modern Wicca there are two basic types of initiation. Let's begin with self-initiation as a concept. Here the idea is that a person can initiate herself or himself into Wicca. Some people conclude that the Goddess and God will bestow initiation upon the sincere seeker when simply asked to do so. There is a fair amount of controversy regarding the authenticity of such a nontraditional approach. If you decide upon using self-initiation in your tradition then you will want to understand the arguments for and against.

In essence, the argument against self-initiation is that a person cannot give himself or herself something that he or she does not already possess. This argument can only be understood by knowing that traditional initiation is bestowed upon a person by an initiator who has the knowledge, experience, and mystical alignments that the initiate is seeking. Therefore, such a person can pass the essence of this energy to the initiate, and thereby align the initiate with the forces that the initiator is already in contact with. This is sometimes referred to as "passing the power."

The counter argument against needing an initiator is that the first initiate in history had no initiator, which seems to indicate that one is not necessary. The return argument is that the first initiate was taught by Otherworld contacts, with which he or she managed to connect. Then, in time, this person brought others to this same contact and from this was born the occult tradition of initiation. The counter argument to this is that the same self-discovery and connection should work today as well. While this is true, we need to understand that in the case of the first initiate, the work of connection was accomplished first, and the stage of being an initiate came after the experience. Therefore, self-initiation, if equated to traditional initiation, cannot be the starting point through a personal rite. It would actually come after the experience and training, and therefore the self-initiation ritual would mark a perceived achievement of being at the traditional initiate level. Fortunately, the means for creating the old Otherworld connections still exist and can be accomplished through the ritual and magical techniques presented in this book.

Now that we have looked at the concept of self-initiation, let's explore the concept of traditional initiation. We have looked at the idea of Otherworld contact and its connection to traditional initiation. Let's explore this a little further by journeying back in time to our distant ancestors.

In our early tribal phase, there were individuals who possessed the ability to connect with spirits and Otherworld realities. These were the shamans, medicine people, and witch doctors common to so-called primitive societies. Many of these people possessed a deep knowledge of plants and their chemical uses. Among these people were the witches, and later the cunningfolk.

Old myths and legends tell of beings, often called faery or elven, who made contact with humans. In the deep quiet woods, and in the silence of the dark night, relationships were formed. Sometimes, according to various tales, an object was given to a human by one of the faery or elven beings. This object possessed magical abilities that allowed the human to accomplish things that he or she could not have previously done.

Over the course of time, the human was either taught or stumbled upon a variety of techniques of a magical nature. These enhanced the ability of the human and manifested such things as oracle power, creating a seer. At some point, the human brought a careful selection of other humans to be taught. Through this, a connective lineage of initiation was established, the essence of which still exists today. It is often referred to as the living chain of memory associations.

The idea of memory chains is that connected ideas carry consciousness up and down the dimensional planes by means of an association chain linked to the vibrations and entities within each dimension. Occult initiation aligns the initiate with these memory chains, and so the chain of associated ideas is connected and awareness is brought through to the subconscious mind of the initiate. This awareness draws the memory of what resides in the other dimensions, and the mind connects with the memory chain associations. The consciousness and the memory begin to share a relationship. However, this is not exactly the same type of memory function through which the mind holds a record of an event. Instead it is linked to the living memory of the chain of connections that lead through and to the nonmaterial dimensions. Once connected, the inner awareness will allow you to perceive things that you have not perceived before. You will see things differently because you are realizing the connection of all things (realization and knowledge are two different things). At this point, the shroud of unawareness that you inherited from societal constraints is lifted and your vision is then opened to expansive new vistas.

The living memory chain is used by nonmaterial spirits, ascended masters, spirit guides, and other beings for communication between the planes. The psychic art of channeling uses the memory chain as well and connects with beings within nonmaterial realms. However, this type of connection is temporary and does not create a sustained connection as does initiation. The concept of the memory chain, and how to use it, will become clearer as the chapter continues, but for now let us continue on the subject of initiation.

Degree System

There are different models of the initiate degree system in Wicca. The most popularized model is the three degree system, which is used largely in the United States. In essence the degrees mark the training periods of basic, intermediary, and advanced. In addition, this often includes a religious "office" association. For example, a second-degree level denotes a priestess or priest, and a third-degree level notes a high priestess or high priest. Not all systems adhere to a standard, and I am not sure we can argue that there actually is one in this eclectic age of modern Wicca.

If you choose to have a degree system in your tradition, it is useful to create corresponding training materials. One model is to establish first degree as the stage at which initiates could learn how to set the altar, cast a circle, and gain a basic understanding of magic and spell casting. The second degree can be set up as an in-depth study period for the theology of your tradition. In addition, the initiates learn more of the ritual and magical arts. In this way, they can conduct or help conduct the rites of your tradition. The third-degree level can be established as the mastery of the ritual and magical arts. In addition, it can be the most significant religious office as marked by the Great Rite, which is the divine marriage. For more information, see the section on the Great Rite in this chapter.

When considering the structure of degrees, think about whether you want to have the initiation level begin the period of training or mark its completion. In other words, will a second-degree initiate in your tradition be already accomplished, or will he or she be just beginning to attain the level of training intended to make one a second-degree initiate? I liken this to martial arts, where a white belt is a novice with no knowledge or experience when he or she begins. However, the next color belt is achieved by first learning the techniques required for the next level, and being able to demonstrate them in a practical display. In this example, a second level belt means that the person can already perform at this level, and is training to meet the requirements of the third level.

Coven Offices

If you want to have a coven structure in your tradition, then you will find it beneficial to establish offices. All organizations have offices and officers, and a smoothly run system requires people working together at different supporting levels. Decide whether the officers are elected or appointed, and whether or not there is a set term of service. You may even want to rotate officers so that everyone can share in the experience. Here are the most common positions:

1. High Priestess or High Priest

2. Priestess or Priest

3. Maiden

5. Guardian

6. Mediator

7. Scribe (Secretary)

8. Treasurer

9. Summoner

The high priestess and high priest are traditionally the directors of the coven or tradition. They oversee the operation of the system and are responsible for providing training and support. In effect, they are actually responsible, or held responsible, for everything that goes on in a coven setting. Outside of this role, they are the spiritual channels that help keep the soul of the coven or tradition alive and integral.

The priestess and priest traditionally aid the high priestess and high priest with teaching and training. They also perform or help perform various rituals of the tradition. Outside of these roles, the priestess and priest are the religious channels that help maintain connection with the deity forms of the tradition. This includes a thorough study of the myths and legends, and the care of statues as well as observation of the days that are sacred to the deities of the tradition (something they share in common with the high priestess and high priest).

The maiden is, in essence, the high priestess' aide. She is traditionally in training to become the high priestess when the time is right. She typically tends the altar during ritual and ensures that supplies are furnished as needed, candles and incense stay lighted, and that the high priestess has what she needs at various stages of the ritual.

The guardian is, in essence, the high priest's aide. He is traditionally in training to become a high priest when his time arrives. He typically helps maintain order during the ritual, keeps a watch on safety factors, and helps with moving people around during initiation rituals. The guardian also assures that the high priest has everything he needs at various points of the ritual.

The mediator of the coven is a trusted and respected person that coven members can go to when problems occur between members of the coven or tradition. They can serve as go-betweens in helping to resolve issues, or can remain neutral and keep the peace during talks while directing the discussion in healthy ways. It is vital that the mediator never takes sides, but instead helps opposing parties hear and understand one another.

The scribe or secretary is responsible for keeping a record of meetings, agreements, rules, laws, and other things that may require recollection or a record. This can include keeping the minutes of a meeting. This should be someone with good writing skills who can also help create ritual text and other things that will be set to paper, disk, or hard drive.

The treasurer is responsible for keeping an account of any money that the coven or tradition acquires. Typically, a fund is collected and kept, from which ritual supplies and other needed items can be purchased. This keeps the financial burden from falling upon any single individual in the coven or tradition. A small amount of money collected monthly from each member should be adequate.

The summoner is a person whose duty it is to let people know the time and place of coven meetings and rituals. The summoner should communicate with everyone to coordinate not only attendance but also who is bringing what. The high priestess and high priest should be able to learn from the summoner exactly who is coming, and that everything is in order for each gathering.

The Eight Fold Path

In traditional Wicca, we find a training program for initiates of the mystery tradition. The Eight Fold Path program is one of the things dropped from mainstream Wicca books during the 1980s as authors presented self-styled teachings, versus time-honored and traditional ones. In essence, the Eight Fold Path represents the traditional eight aspects of magical and religious training, which must be mastered in order to master arts and achieve higher levels of consciousness within the mystery tradition system. Let's examine each of the techniques and methods:

1. Mental discipline through fasting and physical disciplines

2. Development of the will through mental imagery, visualization, and meditation

3. Proper controlled use of drugs that alter the consciousness

4. Personal power, thought-projection, raising and drawing power

5. The keys: ritual knowledge and practice; the use of enchantments, spells, symbols, sigils, and charms

6. Psychic development and dream control

7. Rising upon the planes; astral projection, and mental projection

8. Sex Magic, sensuality, and eroticism

Mental discipline is an important aspect of magical training. It strengthens the will and sharpens the mind of the initiate. The importance of the Wiccan phrase "as my will, so mote it be" stems from the benefits of developing mental fortitude, concentration, and determination. When a trained and accomplished person brings his or her self-discipline and strong will to a ritual or magical intent, then "as my will, so mote it be!" generates a powerful force that seals the intent.

There are a variety of mundane methods that can help a person develop self-discipline. These include such things as yoga, martial arts, dietary regimens, and a routine of physical exercise. Once discipline is achieved, then the personal will of the individual can be further strengthened through a practice of visualization and meditation. One effective exercise involves creating mental images in the mind. For example, you can think of an airplane whose shape and size you are familiar with. Once you have it in your mind, then begin to look at the details of your image. In what direction is the nose of the plane facing? What color is it? How big is it? Look further into its design and note the contours and curves. Can you see the texture of the materials comprising the plane? Performing this exercise with a variety of envisioned objects will help you develop your ability to visualize thought-forms, which are essential for creating astral images that can manifest in the material dimension.

The use of drugs and alcohol is a very controversial subject. There is little doubt that in ancient times alkaloid plants were used by our ancestors, along with ergot mold, to induce trance and altered states of consciousness. In modern Wicca, we still find the presence of ritual wine, which was itself an intoxicant used in the ancient mystery cult of Dionysos. Ritual cakes once contained intoxicating herbal ingredients designed to alter and enhance the mental faculties of the coven members. This may have induced trance states that caused astral projection of the consciousness, allowing the coven to experience Otherworld journeys and astral Sabbats. As with all things in modern Wicca, the individual must decide what is personally appropriate and what is not.

Personal power is an integral part of magical and ritual training in Wicca, and is associated with the ability to draw and raise energy. It is attained through several traditional methods, including participation in each of the eight Sabbats of the year and observing each full moon ritual of the month. Such participation aligns the individuals to lunar- and earth-current energies, which create an energy charge within the aura. The flow of these energies becomes concentrated within a ritual circle, bathing the coven members in a pool of forces swirling in the ritual circle at such occasions as an equinox or solstice. Through these practices, the coven can tap energies that aid the raising of a cone of power (see glossary). Through working with the wand or athame to attract and direct power, the initiate can become proficient at working with energy fields to accomplish a variety of magical and ritual goals.

Learning the various correspondences employed in magic is important to the ritual and magical art. The knowledge of various herbs, enchantments, charms, and spells helps to fine-tune the Wiccan's ability to direct energy. A working knowledge of how and why rituals function helps the Wiccan to focus and to draw upon the momentum of concepts still flowing from out of the past. Like anything in life, practice is required in order to become skillful. You can only be as skilled in the arts as the time and energy you invest in your training exercises.

Psychic development is a very useful tool for the initiate and helps to discern things of a nonphysical nature. This is important because when a person practices magic and ritual, he or she will eventually encounter nonphysical entities. The psychic senses can help to perceive both the presence and the actions of various spirits and elemental creatures. Breathing camphor fumes and drinking rosemary tea (with temperance) when the moon is full will aid in the development of psychic abilities. Dream control is another method that can be employed to train the psychic mind. This involves developing the ability to become conscious in the dream state and then to control and direct the dream as desired (knowing you are doing so).

Astral projection and rising upon the planes are aspects of Wiccan practice designed to allow the Wiccan to access nonphysical realms and states of consciousness. In the ancient mystery sects, it was used to negate the fear of death by proving to the initiate that he or she could still exist outside of the flesh body. The projection of the astral body is something that everyone does while they sleep. It is the dream body that we see in dreams, and its senses allow us to see and to feel while in the dream state. Conscious projection of the mind into the astral body is the ultimate goal of this stage of training. In this way, you can operate in a conscious manner while exploring astral dimensions. (See the suggested reading list for a personal study guide.)

The use of sex magic in Wicca is perhaps an even more controversial subject than the use of drugs and alcohol. At the core of Wicca as an earth religion is the energy of fertility. Sexuality and sensuality were once part of traditional pagan rites intended to ensure a bountiful harvest or a successful hunt. To that end, various levels of sensuality and sexuality were incorporated as a means of raising concentrated energy. In this way, sexual energy served as the *battery* that empowered the old rites. It typically followed erotic dancing and provocative chants. In modern Wicca, many practitioners employ symbolic acts with ritual tools to mimic sexual union. This typically involves the wand (or athame) and chalice. Thus, it is common in Wiccan circles to insert the wand or blade into the chalice, replacing what was once a rite of sexual union.

With the Eight Fold Path system, you now have a guideline for fields of study and practice that can lead you to a mastery of the arts. A personal study of each of these aspects will provide you with the tools through which deeper levels of magical and ritual knowledge can be obtained. Through this, you will possess the keys of a very old and time-proven tradition.

Preserving Tradition

However you ultimately decide to structure your tradition, I believe it is important to factor in the things already preserved in traditional systems. To that end, it is important to know and understand what value such things possess. Once you know this, then you can better understand why they are included. However, in the end, only you can decide what will and will not comprise your tradition.

The value of a cohesive tradition is that it preserves what is connective, functional, and transformative. It teaches time-proven methods that allow an individual to access spiritual energy for personal growth. Its structure provides measured levels of training that weave connections together in the necessary order that leads to the fullness of comprehension. By contrast, eclectic systems shift according to self-directed modes, and have no lasting fibers or threads that maintain connective patterns.

If you want to create an eclectic tradition, then I recommend that you create lasting fibers and threads to anchor your system to a sound foundation. Once the foundation is in place, you can build what you like with little concern for instability. I liken this to saying that you have to build a house in accord with proven methods of sound construction, but no one can tell you how to live your life inside the house. Likewise, how you decorate your home, and what you do with the rooms, is entirely up to you.

A sound tradition provides an established theology. It also contains a practical understanding of magic, a view of the other dimensions, and the knowledge of practical and functional ritual. It connects its members with the momentum of the past, and links them to the vital memory chain associations of its predecessors. These associates are the core concepts and ideas upon which religion, ritual, and magic are founded.

A sound tradition also teaches the differences between religion and spirituality. Religion is the system and mechanism; it is the structure and the process. For example, the establishment of a shrine, the setting of an altar, making offers, and reciting prayers are all religious actions. By contrast, spirituality is the personal connection to divinity; it is the reason why we do religious things. Examples of spirituality include *feeling* the presence of deity, experiencing inner connections, and interfacing with the divine through song, chant, and prayer.

It is in Wicca as a mystery tradition that we find the core memory chains, and the principles that are foundational and vital to the initiate ways. A mystery tradition is a means of preserving key and connective elements that lead to functional levels of enlightenment. Enlightenment leads to far vision, which in turn leads to a glimpse of the world as it is, rather than as we imagined it to be.

The Mystery Tradition

Each mystery tradition is built around its own inner view of the cosmos, which is the microcosm reflecting the higher in the lower. This microcosm contains the connections to higher levels of understanding, and one can include greater evolved beings in this definition as well. Each mystery tradition creates its own symbols, which are fashioned from streams of consciousness that communicate between dimensions.

In Wicca, as a mystery tradition, the myths and legends (along with the hierarchy of deities and spirits) form the setting through which the memory chain becomes accessible. To accomplish this within your own tradition, you will need to be clear about your deities, spirits, and elementals (making sure that their roles and relationships in your tradition are well defined). This is one reason why it is risky to blend cultures—for example, where some of your deities are Celtic and others are Greek. Such pairing may not connect to preestablished memory chains, or may actually short-circuit them.

Once you have your deities, guardians, elements, and other spirits functionally matched and cohesive, then you will need to establish your symbols. Your symbols will be important forms of communication. They maintain the mysteries within a tradition, and no system can sustain itself without them. One example is the pentagram, which symbolizes the harmony of the four creative elements of earth, air, fire, and water.

The symbol tells a story in which the fifth element of spirit brings the four elements out of chaos and into balance. On the pentagram, spirit is assigned to the upper point of the star. Each element is assigned a point of its own. The entire star is enclosed within a circle, which represents the ritual and magical circle of the Craft. The ritual circle is both a container and a barrier, which states that this is about collected and condensed power. The circle, having gates at each of the four quarters, symbolizes access to the outer planes from the inner. Put this all together and the pentagram makes a proclamation to all who behold it (on this plane and the next). It says that the four elements of creation are at your command, and that you possess their cumulative power. It also states that you are under its protection, shielded by energy, and that you can open the portal to other dimensions. To spirits, this is not a symbol, but a reality of the concept in action (just like a cocked gun is not symbolic, but a reality that requires response). They both command attention and state their purpose and power immediately. All traditional Wiccan symbols tell their story and communicate their message. Their stories are old and come from memory chains formed by streams of consciousness. See the chapter on the book of shadows for more information and sample symbols.

The need for a mystery tradition is rooted in the concept of the highest plane or dimension. It is here that what we cannot imagine about divinity and creation exists. This is sometimes called the ultimate plane, which is not only greater than we imagine but also greater than we can imagine at our present mental and spiritual evolution. Within this dimension exists the "Perfect Ideal" in its purity, without diminished expression or emanation. The perfect ideal is the divine blueprint for creation in the hands of the creators (see glossary).

The dimensions that exist within the Universe are active emanations, a communication of what is the divine, what is creation, and the divine plan itself. The material dimension is the lowest vibration of all dimensions. The vibration is so low that energy becomes tangible as a material form. In the material realm, the perception of the perfect ideal is distorted, due to the dense conditions of the material world. It is like looking at a painting through a frosted glass door. Our discernment is distorted by our view.

Occultists of the past created techniques to raise their consciousness into higher planes, where they encountered beings natural to those planes of existence. Some aided the attempt of humankind to rise to a better viewpoint. Those humans who were able to rise through the dimensions became the great spiritual masters. Sometimes this required leaving the physical body behind. In some occult societies, the pathway of ascension to the higher planes is called the Ladder of Light (see glossary).

For the purpose of simplicity, the ladder is depicted with seven rungs, each one symbolizing one of the seven planes of existence. These planes are titled: Ultimate, Divine, Spiritual, Mental, Astral, Elemental, and Physical. Each rung on the ladder of light is a memory chain association that conveys the traveler from the lowest to the highest levels of perception.

Access to the ladder of light, and preservation of the ladder, is essential to the mystery tradition.

Because the ladder of light is a construction of consciousness, it is vital that the mental and spiritual connections remain intact and integral. Any break or any distortion can undo countless centuries of construction. This is why mystery traditions are so strongly opposed to altering the teachings and practices they strive to preserve. Abandoning the established connections can cause us to lose access to the ladder of light, or can dissolve one or more of the ladder's rungs that convey us to the perfect ideal. Restoring it can be quite a feat to undertake.

The mystery tradition and its memory chain associations reside within the classic structure of Wiccan ritual and theology. Under the category of ritual, we can include the following:

1. Ritual Altar: the primary connection to the core of the perfect ideal through its manifestation in the sacred altar setup. The altar is like the keyboard on a computer. The tools and paraphernalia on the altar are the keystrokes and command functions. It is through the altar that we interface with the divine consciousness behind the ritual associations.

2. Elemental Forces: the connection to the divine mind through its creative modes of expression. The elemental forces allow us to join in partnership with the divine formula of creation. In doing so, we reunite our own inner creative essence with the source from which it came. This temporary reunion places us in the stream of divine consciousness as it emanates from the elemental dimension.

3. Four Quarters: the connection to the gateways of direction and communication. The quarters serve as portals that open to various levels of consciousness (both inner and outer). These modes of consciousness touch upon spiritual dimensions through which we can send and receive energy. These gateways are essential to the intent of ritual and magic as they convey the energy toward manifestation.

4. Guardians: the connection to the ushering principles of higher consciousness, which grants access to the ladder of light. The guardians serve as filters, directors, and safeguards that deal with energy. This includes energy sent outward from the circle and energy that streams toward the circle. These entities enforce the *agreement of consciousness* that surrounds a tradition (see glossary). This serves to maintain the internal integrity and ethical foundation of the tradition and its members.

Under the category of theology we can include the following:

1. The Wheel of the Year: the connection to the core cycle of divine expression of the waxing and waning forces within the material world. This is one of the key models of the cycle of return, which is central to Wiccan religion. The wheel provides the internal and external modes of energy that are models for the soul through which it can discern its own seasons of the soul during its material life experience. This is accomplished through an unfolding vision of the divine consciousness in a wholeness of expression.

2. The Triformis Goddess: the connection to the divine principles of life operating through youth, maturity, and old age. It is through the Triple Goddess that we find the inner reflection of our own cycles of evolution. These serve not only as indicators of our progress as souls, but also as directionals that point to awaiting phases. The Triformis Goddess also connects us with the three great realms: Overworld, Middleworld, and Underworld.

3. The Harvest Lord: the connection to the divine principle of birth, life, death, and rebirth. This is another connection very much like the Wheel of the Year, and also related to the Triformis Goddess link, but it is a cycle that is more intimate. Whereas the Wheel of the Year is the soul's journey through a higher cosmic pattern reflected within an earthly model, the Harvest Lord cycle focuses on the reincarnation mysteries within the wheel of rebirth (see glossary). By contrast, the Wheel of the Year unites the soul with

divine consciousness as the whole, while the Harvest Lord cycle directs the soul toward self-awareness as a part of the whole.

4. The Moon Goddess: the connection to the divine expression of the feminine. This is the soul's awareness of the mystical nature. It is the memory of nonmaterial existence and the longing of the soul to return home amidst the stars.

5. The Sun God: the connection to the divine expression of the masculine. This is the soul's awareness of the material realm and its opportunities to teach and reveal the means by which spiritual evolution is accomplished.

6. The Goddess and God consort pair: the connection to the archetype of polarities within divine consciousness. This is the experience of the polarities of divine feminine and masculine consciousness that together provide a glimpse of the divine consciousness in its relative comprehensible expression. It is the soul's memory of wholeness before its isolation in a physical body assigned to a material dimension.

All of the above (in both categories) are ritualized dramatizations and projections of the mystery tradition pattern into various life levels that are experienced in the material dimension.

By incorporating all of these elements into your tradition, you can create and sustain the necessary links to the perfect ideal. How you structure your tradition will not adversely affect these alignments and interface points as long as you incorporate them all into a cohesive and practical system. This is because the formula is what is important.

In effect, the formula establishes a practical conscious relationship between the initiate and the divine consciousness from which the memory chain associations form the ladder of light. The function of the mystery tradition is to provide the means by which the initiates can form reaction patterns, which will result in spiritual development on the inner levels. The mystery teachings and structure provide this means by applying the effective stimulus in the required degree. This is measured out through the prescribed rituals and the cohesive formulation of the mystery tradition's theology. As noted earlier, this is one of the primary reasons why the initiate systems of the mystery tradition resist any changes to the established construction of its tradition.

Egregores

The concept of the *Egregore* (also known as a *Telesmic*) is important to the mystery tradition. An egregore is a mental image, usually of a being, that is constructed on the astral plane. In the mystery tradition, it is created in such a way that it draws archetypical energy to it. This, in turn, allows for the downpouring of divine consciousness into the egregore, which then becomes sentient. This is not unlike the concept of a soul dwelling in a physical body. While the soul may be living the life of John Smith this time around, it is not John Smith, nor is it not John Smith. It is, instead, a shared consciousness of two projections.

An egregore is, in effect, part human construction and part divine consciousness. From the perspective of the mystery traditions, the various gods of myth and legend are egregore forms. The deities and entities associated with Wicca, from the perspective of the mystery tradition, are representations of types of consciousness not reachable by other means. By personifying them, humans can attain and access the levels of actuality, as opposed to the envisioned or imagined. In other words, the initiate can make direct contact with the consciousness behind the projected image or pattern as it truly is on a higher dimension. The quality of such contacts is, of course, in direct proportion to the spiritual evolution of the initiate who makes the contact.

One of the secrets of the mystery teachings is that truth is found through the false, or literally "truth is found in the heart of a lie." To explain this, we need to look at the old formulations. The structure of the ancient mystery traditions evolved through a conscious effort to understand and map out the unknown. This involved the evolution of concepts related to forces, spirits, deities, and the unexplainable. When one model that previously served our understanding eventually collapsed under new evidence or experience, it was shifted to another and then to another until it maintained itself through the test of time. This is just like the methodology used in science.

In science, the scientist operates upon the idea that her or his knowledge is considered to be true and accurate (although she or he may state that such and such is the current belief). Over the course of time scientists have had to abandon certain things that proved no longer true or functional. The same thing is true of historians. In these examples, we find that the methodology is what is true, but not always the conclusions. It is only because something is proven false that we come closer to knowing what is true. So too was it with the ancients who created the mystery tradition methodology.

The initiate of the mysteries understands that nothing is false or inaccurate unless a truth exists to render it so. Therefore, he or she understands that the images and forms used in the mystery tradition are not flawless. But the initiate also knows that they serve to connect with what is empirical through the connection made to the consciousness that actually animates the form or image. Therefore, the initiate is not disturbed with thoughts of the existence or nonexistence regarding the things of the mystery tradition. Instead, she or he relies upon the reality of the divine consciousness behind the forms and images, which connect the initiate with the actualities of the consciousness that they represent.

Sacred Rites

Among the sacred rituals of Wicca, there are three that are most represented in Wiccan literature. Two of them fall under the category of lunar rites. These are Drawing Down the Moon, and the rite of Cakes and Wine. In the mystery tradition these concepts contain deeper levels than the concepts commonly portrayed in most published books.

The third sacred ritual is known as the Great Rite, and it is the most controversial of the three Wiccan rituals. The Great Rite traditionally includes a sexual union, which is performed as part of the third-degree initiation ceremony. In some cases, the Great Rite may be performed in conjunction with the higher levels of sex magic practices or rituals.

Let us now examine each of these rites as they appear in the mystery tradition:

1. CAKES AND WINE is part of the divine meal ritual, which takes place near the end of the full moon rite and in some seasonal rituals. It is a rite that is intimately connected to the Harvest Lord and Earth Goddess mysteries. Its purpose is to unite the inner divine spark of the ritualist with the source through which it was generated. This is accomplished through the use of a ritual cake and a drink of wine, which are specially prepared for the rite.

The cake is made from grains, traditionally barley, but wheat is also often used instead. The grain is associated with myths of the Underworld and of the mysteries of the unknown. The mythos is established around the agricultural year wherein the seed is planted in the darkness of the earth and buried. There it remains, and from a mystical perspective receives the teachings of the Underworld. Afterward, the seed breaks through to the light of the mortal world and imparts the teachings to the plant. New seeds are produced and then harvested. The seeds are made into cakes, which then contain the inner mysteries. They represent the body of the Slain Harvest Lord, and when eaten they impart their secrets to the inner spirit of the person consuming the meal.

The wine is made from dark grapes, growing in clusters that resemble the multi-breasted image of Diana of Ephesus. The grapes are associated with myths of fertility and divine intoxication. The transformation of the grape into juice and the period of fermentation are associated with the menstrual cycle of women and the gestation period of human pregnancy. In this regard, the wine symbolizes the magical life blood of the Goddess. When the mystical essence is consumed, it imparts the cyclical life essence and the properties of transformation to the person drinking the wine.

The ritual of Cakes and Wine is also known as the divine meal. Traditionally, this is presented to the initiate by the high priestess and high priest, who say:

> Through this cake and by this wine may you come to know that
> which in you is of the eternal gods.

The initiate eats a portion of the cake and drinks a portion of the wine. Through this ritual act, the initiate is united with the Source of All Things on an inner and outer level. It is in this union that the divine spark (the indwelling soul of the initiate) is joined in a moment of light with its creators.

2. DRAWING DOWN THE MOON in modern Wicca is designed to attract the consciousness of the Goddess into the mind, spirit, and body of a high priestess during the ritual of the full moon. The older form of the rite, in ancient times, involved drawing down the mystical force of the light of the full moon to the earth. This held a different meaning, but ultimately connected with the same divine consciousness.

The most common purpose for this ritual is to provide an oracle. It is also used on occasions where serious problems arise and the channeled consciousness of the Goddess is required. In either case, the woman receiving the downpouring of feminine divine consciousness needs to be experienced in receiving and handling this type of possession.

The basic technique involves first attaining what occultists call the *Nil* state of consciousness. This means thinking of nothing and allowing the mind to become a still and quiet pool. Into this night-like darkness and quietness, the woman visualizes an X and then assumes the posture by raising and spreading her arms upward and outward. Her feet are also spread widely, resulting in her body's formation of an X.

**Figure 7: Drawing Down the Moon Posture
shown with Astronomical Associations**

In the next step of Drawing Down the Moon the woman visualizes the X again, but this time mentally adds a V over the top of it. This creates the ancient symbol of the chevron, which often appears in conjunction with female symbolism and iconography in prehistoric art. Once this symbol is fully visualized, the woman slowly raises her chin upward, which gently forces the head back. This is a sign of readiness to the high priest who kneels before her.

The high priest raises the ritual wand and lightly presses the tip to the three sacred points on the body of the female vessel of the Goddess. These points are the nipples and the genital area, which collectively symbolize the nurturing and generative forces of the feminine. It is from this power that all things issue forth and are sustained in the early portion of their manifestation. Therefore it is through this principle that the Goddess manifests through the woman in this ritual.

Once the purpose of the rite is completed, then the woman dissolves the connection. This is accomplished by the woman once again taking up the X position and then visualizing the full moon around her body. Next, she slowly lowers her arms to her side, visualizing the moon beginning to wane. Finally, she draws her feet back together as she completes the visualization of the moon completely disappearing. This places the woman back in the inner darkness of the Nil state of consciousness. All that is required at this stage is for the woman to inhale and exhale deeply three times, open her eyes, and return fully conscious to the setting around her. A snack and drink should be given to the woman at this time, as this helps her return to normalcy.

The coven scribe can keep records of such events, recording the date and what was conveyed by the Goddess through the woman.

3. THE GREAT RITE is a ritual through which the participants invoke the Nil consciousness, which is then temporarily filled with the downpouring of the divine feminine and masculine consciousness. This ritual is also known as the *Heiros Gamos,* or divine marriage.

As noted earlier, the Great Rite is part of the traditional third-degree initiation. In this context, the ritual is intended to wed the initiate with the divine gender polarity that is opposite her or his own gender. In other words, a man is wedded to the Goddess and a woman wedded to the God. The wedding is, of course, metaphorical and denotes the level required to act as a representative of deity within a ritual setting. This is something that a high priestess and a high priest must do on occasion.

A relatively new type of Great Rite exists in which the joining of divine gender polarities is symbolized rather than experienced through physical intimacy. This involves substituting the ritual chalice for the feminine aspect and the wand for the masculine (some systems use the athame). The chalice is raised by the high priestess and the wand is lowered into it by the high priest (in some systems the tools are in the hands of the opposite gender association).

Now that we have examined the elements and aspects that empower a tradition and provide for spiritual and magical growth, we can turn to a means of recording them for future use. In the next chapter we will explore the book of shadows and look at a variety of symbols and other factors used in the ritual and magical art of Wicca.

eight

THE BOOK OF SHADOWS

The book of shadows is a classic component of traditional and mainstream Wicca. In its earliest references, the book was, in essence, a record of rituals, beliefs, practices, and recipes of various types. Sometime after the early 1980s, the book of shadows took on the additional form of a diary or personal journal. In many contemporary cases this form now constitutes the majority of the books of shadows (particularly for solitary practitioners). For the purposes of this chapter, I will deal mainly with the traditional structure. I believe this will provide a good foundation for the consideration of how you wish to organize your book. After looking this over, you can easily decide how traditional or how informal you want to make the book of shadows for your own system.

Traditionally, people were allowed to copy from a book of shadows once they had received initiation. The book, while belonging to a high priestess or high priest, was available to the coven members as part of their personal training. The copying process was closely observed in order to guard against copying errors. Today many of these books were not copied from a teacher's book of shadows, but instead are self-creations (although they are often based upon published works).

There is an oral tradition that the book of shadows originally did not possess any words because at one time literacy was not widespread among the common people. It is said that the book contained instructional symbols and pictographs, which each student memorized. In this way, ritual information and magical technique was passed along from teacher to student. The books were read and copied at night by candlelight or in front of the hearth. Shadows washed across the pages and from this the nickname "book of shadows" originated. This is one of several tales regarding the origin of the name.

The classic book of shadows begins with an opening page upon which appears an admonishment against any ill use of the book. If you wish to include this, you can use words to this effect:

> This book is under the protection of the magic it weaves. Be forewarned that if you should misuse it, all will turn back upon you thrice. In the names of the Goddess and God, so mote it be!

For something with a gentle tone, you can use the following text:

> Harm ye none by the ways within,
> not enemy nor closest kin.
> The law is to live and to let live,
> you shall receive what you shall give.

For something more daunting, you may wish to use this text:

> Be it known unto all that this book is under the protection of the Old Ones who were from before time itself. If you misuse this book, or steal this book, then shall all the arts you cherish turn against you. Then shall you be left to the mercy of the Dread Lords of the Outer Spaces.

Once you have written the text on the page, place the binding symbol (figure 8) beneath the words in the center of the page:

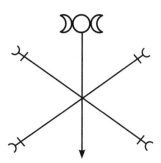

Figure 8: Book of Shadows Binding Sigil

Figure 9: Guardian Pentagram

Immediately following the opening page of text is the traditional pentagram seal, which is on a separate page of its own (figure 9). This seal bears the symbols of the following spirits (from top and moving clockwise): Abdia, Ballaton, Bellony, Halliy, and Halliza. In the center is the spirit Soluzen. These spirits have power and influence over the ritual and magical arts, and also serve as protectors of the book of shadows and its contents.

Once the symbols are drawn in your book, trace the pentagram with your athame. Begin by touching the top point of the star and then tracing in a clockwise manner. End by touching the center. Each line of the pentagram corresponds with one of the verses (the final verse is recited when the athame is pressed to the center):

> Light and darkness bring the shadow's edge,
> Oaths preserve the ancestral pledge.
> Whispers of Old Ones in the deep dark woods,
> Voices known only to the wearers of hoods.
> Here are the secrets received in the night,
> Kept now in this record of thrice sacred rite.

Next, take your athame and trace the spirit symbols, speaking each name before you trace the corresponding symbol. Once all the names have been spoken, place the palms of both hands over the pentagram and say:

> Pen and ink to mark the rites,
> Drawn from moonlight in the night.
> Guardian eyes that always look,
> Protect all things within this book.

Now the book is ready to write your rituals in, and for the placement of the symbols, signs, and gestures of the art.

The Book of Shadows Order of Appearance

1. The Tools of the Art: In this section, place images and/or a list and description of the tools used in your tradition. Include any symbols or designs that are etched or painted on the tools. These will also be included in another section of the book. If there is any special lore associated with the tools, then include this as well.

2. Alphabet or Runic Script: The book of shadows that was a feature of Wicca in the mid-twentieth century contained a script known as Theban, or as the Witches' Alphabet. The inclusion of a mys-

tical or secret alphabet is classic within traditions that employ a grimoire of one type or another. You may wish to use the Theban script or another system in your tradition.

3. Ritual Signs and Gestures: In this section, place drawings or photos of the ritual hand signs, body postures, or anything of this nature. These signs and gestures enhance communication and allow the mind to work on two different levels at the same time: mundane and mystical.

4. Ritual Incense and Oils: This section will include the types of oils and herbs used in your tradition. You may want to arrange them into magical and ritual uses and correspondences. This is also the place to keep recipes used to create the oils and incense.

5. How to Cast a Circle: In this section, place the preparation of a ritual setting, the method of casting a circle, and the means by which the circle is dissolved after the rite is completed.

6. Rites of Initiation: This section will contain the rituals for dedication as well as the degree system you choose to use in your tradition. Also include a reference list for needed supplies used in each rite. This will save you time looking it up in another section.

7. Lunar Rites: In this section, record the moon rituals. These can include dark moon, waxing moon, full moon, and waning moon. Also record any special lore related to the moon in this section.

8. Sabbat Rituals: This section will contain all the eight Sabbat rituals. Decide where in the Wheel of the Year you wish to begin the calendar, and then begin with the ritual of that season. Keep the rituals in the order of appearance from that ritual forward, as this will make it easier to turn to the seasonal ritual that you desire.

9. Spells and Works of Magic: In this section, record the spells and works of magic that have proven effective. You may wish to group them into categories for easy reference, such as love spells, prosperity spells, healing spells, spells of protection, and so forth.

10. Ritual and Magical Correspondences: This section will contain lists and charts of the correspondences used in your rituals, spells, and works of magic. You may wish to group them into categories such as colors, stones, herbs, planets, animals, stars, chakras, and so on.

11. Recipes: In this section, place any recipes for cakes, cookies, drinks, and other things that are used for the celebrations in your tradition.

12. Personal Journal: This section can contain any personal things that you want to record and pass on to others. This is your story and can be of value to those who practice your tradition in the future.

The Traditional Tools

In Wicca, we commonly find the four traditional tools of Western Occultism: the pentacle, wand, athame, and chalice. To enhance your book of shadows, you can add drawings or photos of the tools, accompanied by any symbols you wish to use with each tool. Symbols on the tools bring a special quality to them, and provide for an air of mystery or secrecy. Such things aid in the arousal of an altered state of consciousness during ritual or magical procedures. This is because symbols speak directly to the subconscious mind as well as to the conscious mind. In this regard, symbols are the language between the worlds.

The use of ritual tools similar to those found in Wicca is very ancient. One example appears in the ancient cult of Mithras. Here we find the wand of command, the libation cup, a crescent-shaped knife, and a platter (a type of pentacle). Also included was the sun sword, which, when added to the other tools, gives us a set very much like those of Gardnerian Wicca.

Another depiction of the four tools, in an occult setting, appears in the reconstructed card of the Magician from the fifteenth-century Italian tarot set now known as the Cary-Yale Visconti deck. The Magician stands before a table set with the pentacle, wand, chalice, and dagger.

Figure 10: The Four Tools

These elemental tools are available to the Magician to use in the art of magic and ritual. With the exception of the chalice, this classic set of tools also appears together as ritual items in the *Key of Solomon*.

The four tools used in Wicca constitute a set of spiritual implements for religious and ritual purposes as well as mystical tools for magical works. Some occultists assign certain virtues to the ritual tools. The pentacle is the shield of valor. The wand is the lance of intuition. The athame is the sword of reason, and the chalice is the well of compassion. In such a view the four tools become the weapons of the spiritual knight, which we noted in the chapter on ritual construction.

The following illustrations of the tools and their symbols can be used as a model for designing your own set:

Figure 11: The Pentacle (with Symbols)

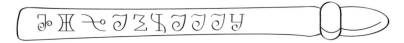

Figure 12: The Wand (with Symbols)

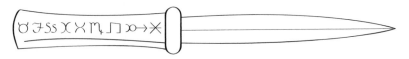

Figure 13: The Athame (with Symbols)

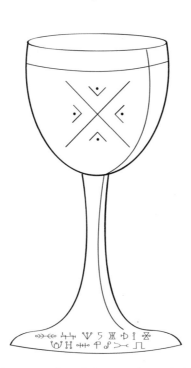

Figure 14: The Chalice (with Symbols)

The Theban Script

Traditionally, many systems used an alphabet known as the Theban Script or Witches' Alphabet. It was used to keep the text in the book of shadows secret so that prying eyes could not read the material. The use of secret alphabets was, and is, very common within secret societies. Wicca was one such society up until its public exposure by Gerald Gardner.

The earliest known reference to the Theban alphabet appears in Cornelius Agrippa's sixteenth-century masterpiece known as the *Three Books of Occult Philosophy*. Agrippa is acknowledged today as one of the greatest occult minds of his time period. He lived in Italy from 1512–1515 and studied the writings of Marsilio Ficino and Pico de la Mirandola, who translated the great Hermetic texts of ancient Greek and Egyptian occultism.

According to occult tradition, the Theban alphabet originated in the ancient Greek city of Thebes, hence the name. Some people attribute its later popularity to the book known as the *Sworn Book of Honorius*, also known as *The Grimoire of Honorius*. The ancient appearance of the Theban script in the Aegean/Mediterranean and its modern appearance in Wicca suggest a borrowing from southern Europe.

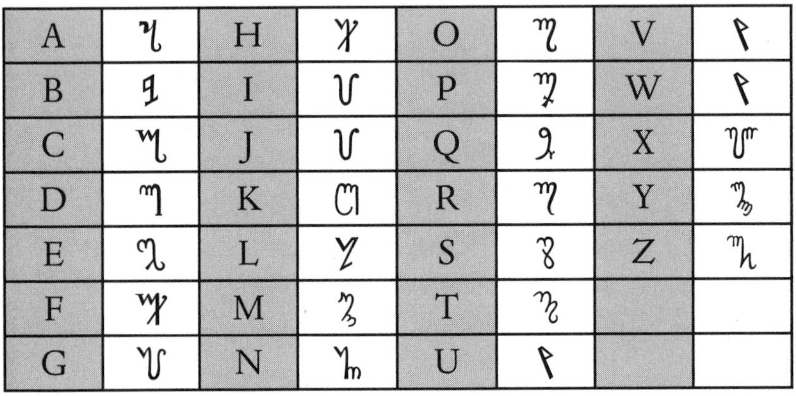

A	ʮ	H	Ꙩ	O	ᴍ	V	Ꝑ
B	ꝯ	I	Ʊ	P	ᵑ	W	Ꝑ
C	ᵚ	J	Ʊ	Q	ꝯ	X	Ʊᵐ
D	ᵐ	K	Ꝏ	R	ᵑ	Y	ᵑ
E	ꝙ	L	Ɏ	S	ꝣ	Z	ᵐ
F	ᵚᶌ	M	ꝧ	T	ᵑ		
G	Ꝩ	N	ᵑ	U	Ꝑ		

Figure 15: Theban Script

Ritual Signs and Gestures

It is more than likely that the earliest form of human communication, prior to words and sounds, was the use of hand gestures and body postures. Among the American tribes, sign language was used between tribes that spoke different languages, which shows a widespread knowledge of gestures as an independent form of communication. There can be no argument that sign language is vital for the deaf and mute.

In occult tradition, the use of signs and gestures has a long history. Their use is designed to communicate in both realms during ritual and magical work. In other words, such communication is directed toward the ritualists within the circle and the entities outside of the circle. If we think about the old saying that "a picture is worth a thousand words," we can begin to understand the importance of signs and gestures. In this light, they can quickly convey entire concepts and communicate directions without uttering a single word. This helps maintain silence in a ritual setting, enhancing the air of mystery and sense of magic.

The following signs and gestures are among the most common found in modern Wicca. They come from a variety of occult sources:

Figure 16: Triple Goddess Gesture

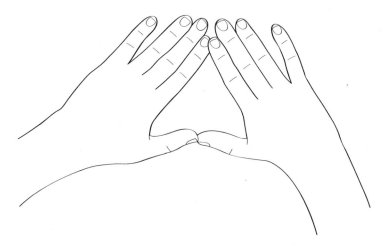

Figure 16A: Triangle of Manifestation

Figure 17: Banishing Gesture

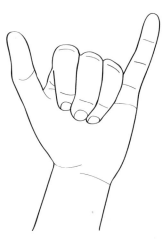

**Figure 17A: Horned God (with the right hand),
Crescent Crowned Goddess (with the left hand)**

Figure 18: Goddess Posture

Figure 18A: God Posture

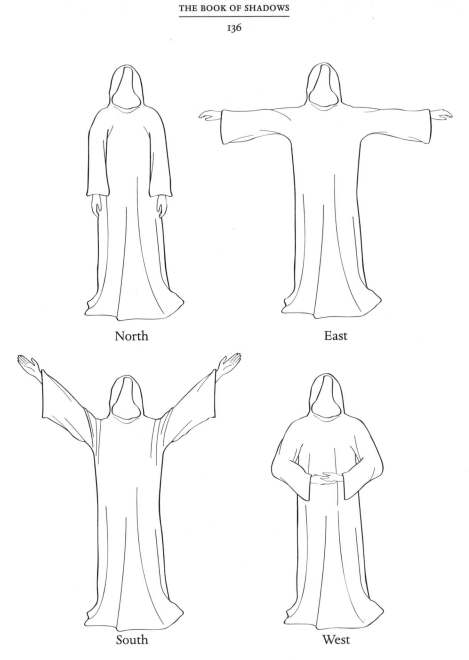

North

East

South

West

Figure 19: Four Quarters Ritual Postures

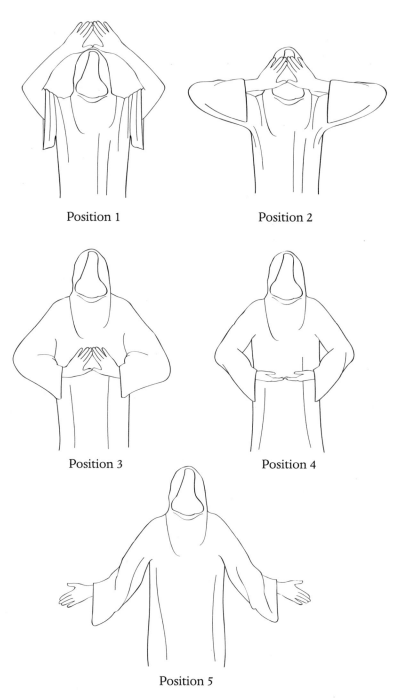

Position 1   Position 2

Position 3   Position 4

Position 5

Figure 20: Rite of Union

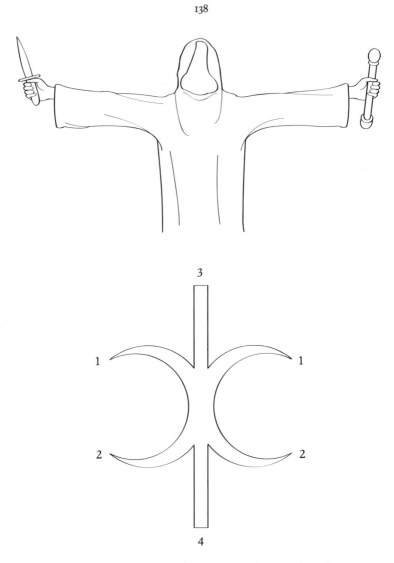

Figure 21: Gesture of Power, showing numbered placements to direct sequence of movements

Wiccan Symbols

In Wicca, symbols can be used for a variety of purposes. They can be used as a script to define the use of a tool, in which case they are marked upon it. They can be used to denote a concept, convey a magical principle, or simply indicate an association. The following symbols are among the most common:

Ritual Circle	Four Elements	The Watchers
The Goddess	The God	Elementals
First Degree	Second Degree	Third Degree

Figure 22: Ceremonial Symbols

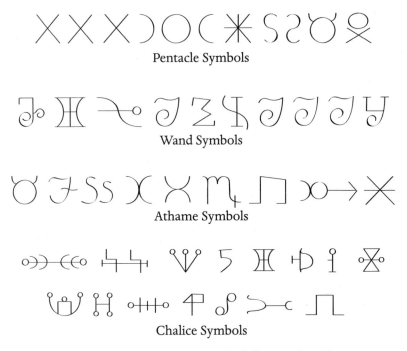

Pentacle Symbols

Wand Symbols

Athame Symbols

Chalice Symbols

Figure 23: Classic Wiccan Symbols for Ritual Tools

Figure 24: Ritualist Symbolism as Master of the Circle

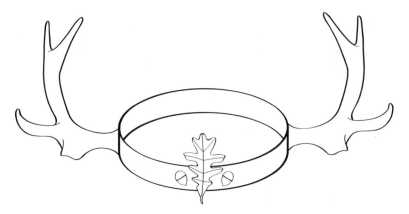

**Figure 25: Rustic Woodland Goddess Headpiece
worn by High Priestess on Crossquarters**

**Figure 26: Woodland Sun God Headpiece
worn by High Priest on Solstice and Equinox**

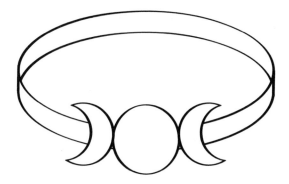

Figure 27: High Priestess Headpiece

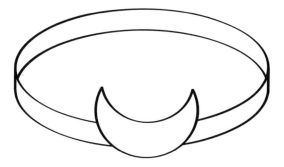

Figure 28: Priestess Headpiece

Ritual Altar and Circle Setup

As previously mentioned, the altar and ritual represent the mini-universe of the ritualist. Both are constructed in accord with occult principles that reflect the perfect ideal from which creation of the Universe arose. The circle is set between the worlds and the altar at its center fixes and holds it in place. The altar becomes the center of balance for the four elements that flank all four sides.

There are several different ways to set an altar. Your altar can be anything from a simple devotional altar to a complex ceremonial magic altar. When it comes to most rituals, you will find it useful to have at least some basics in place. These include candles (to symbolize something and to provide lighting), incense, four elemental representations, a bowl of water and some salt, deity representations, and your ritual tools. On a mundane level you will also want to have some matches on hand, along with something with which to snuff out the candles. A utility knife is also handy to have.

In the mystery tradition, the altar is set with specific objects in a particular way, putting into place the various alignments that activate the vital states of consciousness. This makes the altar a type of battery that generates energy during the entire ritual.

In another chapter we noted the black altar cloth, which symbolizes the darkness of procreation from which all things issue forth. This is included in the mystery altar, which is also set with other symbolic objects that connect to metaphors. The illustration shows the basic setup, which can be embellished as needed in accord with the intent of the ritual or work of magic.

Looking at the illustration, note the presence of a candle in the center of the altar. Behind and off to each side are two other candles. Together, all three candles form a triangle, with the tip of the triangle closest to the front of the altar. This triangle configuration symbolizes the downpouring of divine consciousness. The candle at this tip of the triangle is surrounded by four bowls, which are the elemental representations.

The configuration of the elemental bowls around the candle signify the harmony of earth, air, fire, and water when brought into balance by

Figure 29: Mystery Tradition Altar Setup

the light of spirit, which is the fifth element. It is here that you interface with the five streams of consciousness flowing from the Otherworld.

To the left of the elemental bowls is a container of salt water for purification of the ritual circle area. To the right of the elemental bowls is a censer with smoking incense. The intent of the smoke is two-fold. It serves as a medium in which nonmaterial entities can reside in the material realm during the ritual, and it conveys the intent of the rituals as it rises up and leaves the circle.

Returning for a moment to the triangle of candles, you will note that on the center is a skull figure. The skull symbolizes ancestral wisdom; it is what remains behind as generations disappear from the material realm. On top of the skull is a candle that, when lighted, symbolizes the active connection to the ancestral group mind.

Looking again at the illustration, you will notice goddess and god images next to the candles in the back area of the altar. The Goddess image is set to the left and the God image is placed on the right. In basic occultism, these placements represent the polarities of divinity in gender expression. The God polarity is active and electrical. The Goddess polarity is receptive and magnetic. The directions of left and right are assigned these traits as well.

It is at the center of the altar that the vortex of energy appears and functions at its most intense. Whatever is placed on the center of the altar becomes the point of alignment to the elemental realm. It also establishes a portal or gateway between the worlds and the inner planes. In the mystery tradition, fire always occupies the center as it was the earliest of divine images, and in occult tradition it establishes the presence of the fifth element upon the altar.

Placing the ritual pentacle beneath the candle directly establishes an open connection between the material dimension and the nonmaterial dimension. It is a ritual sign indicating "as above, so below." From this point on, everything performed in the ritual (each vibration and emanation of energy) will be drawn into the center of the altar. From here, it will flow into the elemental portals. Once amplified by the elements, the ritual intent will be drawn into the astral substance where it will take on a representation in form. This is the principle of the generated thought-form described in an earlier chapter.

All of the symbolism incorporated into an altar setting is very important. In part, it will evoke and invoke certain alignments associated with the symbolism. Therefore, it is important to arrange the altar accordingly. The alignments that you create will affect your ritual and your magic (for better or for worse).

The use of colors is vital to the attraction and direction of mystical forces, and they serve as forms of communication in the same manner as any symbolism. This is reflected in the black altar cloth that represents the procreative darkness that existed before creation was generated through the perfect ideal. The center candle on the altar represents the "Great Unmanifest" at the center of nothingness. The two Goddess and God candles represent the first manifestations of definable consciousness that arise from the Source of All Things. The Goddess candle is red and the God candle is black—the meaning of these colors will become evident as we proceed.

A black candle is set on the head of the skull and is lighted for all rituals performed from the Autumn Equinox until the Spring Equinox. A red candle is used from the Spring Equinox until the Autumn Equinox. Black symbolizes the ancestral knowledge retained within the source, the realm of the Otherworld. Red symbolizes the ancestral knowledge that flows from the Otherworld to the world of mortals.

During the course of the year, the color of the skull's candle will match either the Goddess or God candle. Black represents the secret shadow realm, the deep dark forest, and the mystical journey that leads to the Otherworld. The God is the escort who aids in transition of the dead.

Red represents the life blood, the inner pulse that sustains and empowers. Regarding the Goddess, it runs through the earth beneath the soil, for she is the giver of life. Red symbolizes the place of life and renewal, which is reflected in the menstrual blood cycle. In the context of the skull figure, red symbolizes the ancient knowledge flowing into the world of the living from the source of its wellspring.

To better align with the ancestral memory, a small cauldron is placed in front of the skull. This represents the Moon gate, which is the womb of the Goddess. Through the Goddess, all things are birthed from the Otherworld and return to her again. Therefore, the cauldron leads to and from the ancestral knowledge. Because of this, it contains the magical essence of transformation.

The remaining tools of the Craft are now placed on the altar in association with their quarter element. The wand is set in the east portion of the altar. The athame occupies the southern section, and the chalice is set in the west area. The pentacle has been previously set in the center beneath the candle. The altar itself is oriented to the east, meaning that the practitioner is facing east as he or she views the altar.

Now that we have looked at the basic layout for a book of shadows, we can consider one last element to complete your tradition. This will require compiling a list of correspondences. Let's turn to the next chapter and look at some foundational listings.

nine

THE CORRESPONDENCES

No system or tradition is complete without an assignment of ritual and magical correspondences. The prepared correspondences make it easier to compile the necessary components with which to construct a ritual or spell. Whenever you need to design a ritual or spell, the first things to consider are the symbolic elements that will empower and drive the ritual.

When creating your own spells, or embellishing ones that already exist, it is important to consider any correspondences related to the work at hand. Go over the list in this chapter and incorporate as much as possible. Consider the numerical value of the planet that rules over the spell's intent. An example of this might be to add seven roses to a spell for love, since seven is the number of the planet Venus, and roses are sacred to the goddess Venus.

Remember that colors, scents, and symbols are all necessary, as they stimulate the senses of the person casting the spell. This stimulation creates a vibration, which then causes a reaction within the subconscious mind, then in turn within the etheric substance of the astral plane. As we know from the law of physics, every action causes a reaction. So it is also with the law of metaphysics.

Most rituals will need a deity, ritual tool, quarter direction, color, scent, symbolic totems, and a power object. These are basics to which you can add other enhancements. The following lists of correspondences can serve as is, or as models from which you can create what makes sense to your own tradition.

1. Ritual and Magical Correspondences

Planetary Colors:

> *Sun:* Gold or Yellow
>
> *Moon:* White
>
> *Mars:* Red
>
> *Mercury:* Violet
>
> *Jupiter:* Blue
>
> *Venus:* Green
>
> *Saturn:* Black

Color Symbolism—Spell Casting:

> *White:* Purification, protection
>
> *Pink:* Love, friendship
>
> *Yellow:* Drawing (pulling/compelling)
>
> *Green:* Material success, abundance
>
> *Red:* Passion, vigor, sexual energy
>
> *Orange:* Concentration, psychic energy
>
> *Purple:* Power over obstacles, magical forces
>
> *Brown:* Neutralizing
>
> *Gold:* Drawing (strengthens other candles)
>
> *Blue:* Peace, spirituality, spiritual energy
>
> *Dark Blue:* Depression
>
> *Black:* Crossing, suppressing, ending

Ritual Color Symbolism:

  White: Purity, transmitting

  Green: Nature magic, love, receptive fertility

  Blue: Peace, spiritual forces

  Red: Life force, sexual energy, vitality, active fertility

  Brown: Earth magic, neutralizing/grounding

  Yellow: Mental energy

  Black: Drawing, absorbing

Elemental Associations:

There are two basic sets of color correspondence for the elements. The following is the oldest set:

  Earth: (Yellow) Strength, fortitude—elemental beings called Gnomes

  Air: (Blue) Intellect, healing, freeing, inspiration—elemental beings called Sylphs

  Fire: (Red) Sexual energy, lifegiving, cleansing, force, desire—elemental beings called Salamanders

  Water: (green) Emotion, subconscious, love, fertility, adaptability—elemental beings called Undines

In the old set, yellow symbolizes the sun's warmth, which aids the growth cycle of plants in the soil. Blue is the color of the sky. Red is the color of intensely heated objects. Green is the color of the sea associated with storms, which reflect the active power of water versus the passive color (blue).

Many modern Wiccan traditions use a newer set of associations, which follow here:

  Earth: Green

  Air: Yellow

  Fire: Red

  Water: Blue

In the newer system, green represents fertility (the growth of trees and plants). Blue is the sky, and red is the heat of fire. Blue is associated with the color of the calm ocean. The assignment of elemental spirit names is the same in the old an new systems.

Ritual Tool Correspondences:

Pentacle: Earth (feminine quality)

Wand: Air (masculine quality)

Athame: Fire (masculine quality)

Chalice: Water (feminine quality)

Quarter Correspondences:

North: Power—element of earth—guardian Boreas

East: Persuasion—element of air—guardian Eurus

South: Force—element of fire—guardian Notus

West: Adaptation—element of water—guardian Zephyrus

Aromatics:

Sun: Cinnamon, laurel, oilbanum

Moon: Almond, jasmine, camphor, lotus

Mars: Aloes, dragon's blood, tobacco

Mercury: Cinquefoil, fennel, aniseed

Jupiter: Nutmeg, juniper, basil

Venus: Myrtle, rose, ambergris

Saturn: Myrrh, poppy, asafoetida

Numbers:

1. Primal, central, fortitude

2. Polarity, balance, harmony

3. Mystical, formational, uniting

4. Ambition, innovative

5. Action, friction, challenge

6. Force, power, energy

7. Completion, success

8. Diversity, expansion, freeing

9. Occult forces, veiled, magical, unrevealed

Numbers & Associated Planets:

Sun: 6

Moon: 9

Mars: 5

Mercury: 8

Jupiter: 4

Venus: 7

Saturn: 3

2. Plant and Mineral Kingdom Correspondences

Wicca, as a Nature religion, embraces the plant and mineral kingdom in its magical arts. This is why we find an abundance of spells containing herbs, stones, and trees. Nature or earth magic is an integral part of the Wiccan's Craft. The following list of correspondences will provide you with the most traditional items.

Trees and Planetary Associations:

Sun: Laurel and oak

Moon: Willow, olive, palm

Mars: Hickory

Mercury: Hazel

Jupiter: Pine, birch, mulberry

Venus: Myrtle, ash, apple

Saturn: Elm

Stones & Planetary Associations:

Sun: Diamond, topaz

Moon: Moonstone, opal, clear crystal quartz

Mars: Bloodstone, ruby, jasper

Venus: Emerald, green tourmaline, aquamarine

Jupiter: Amethyst, chrysocolla, chrysoprase

Mercury: Chalcedony, citrine

Saturn: Black onyx, jet, black jade

Herbs & Planetary Associations:

Sun: Peony, angelica, sunflower, saffron, cinnamon, laurel, wolfsbane

Moon: Selenotrope, hyssop, rosemary, watercress, moonflower,
moonwort, garlic

Jupiter: Basil, mint, elecampane, henbane, betony, sage

Venus: Lavender, vervain, valerian, coriander, laurel, lovage,
foxglove

Mars: Wolfsbane, hellebore, garlic, tobacco, capsicum

Saturn: Dragon's wort, rue, cummin, hellebore, mandrake,
aconite, hemlock

Mercury: Fennel, mint, smallage, marjoram, parsley

3. Correspondences of Trees, Plants, and Stones

Trees:

Alder: Associated with oracle properties. In ancient lore, it is also a guardian tree set at the gateway to the Otherworld.

Apple: Associated with love and healing. It is also a faery tree, and in ancient lore, a branch provides safe passage in and out of the Otherworld.

Ash: Associated with divinatory properties. It is also known as the World tree, and in ancient lore was a bridge between the mortal realm and the Otherworld.

Beech: Associated with ancient knowledge, and in ancient lore is favored by the elven beings. The beech is also known as the Mother tree, and is associated with feminine mystique. The etymology of the beech is traceable to the Anglo-Saxon word *boc*, and the German word *buch*, which can be translated into the English word *book*. Historically, thin slices of beech were used to make books in ancient times.

Birch: Associated with banishing evil spirits, purification, protection, and binding. In ancient lore, it is also associated with safe passage within the Otherworld.

Elder: Associated with faery doorways. In ancient lore, it granted the power of shape-shifting, and possessed the power to transform in general.

Elm: Associated with gateways into the Otherworld. In ancient lore, it was associated with the Underworld as a type of bridge. The elm is considered especially sacred to the elven beings, and some commentators claim that the name is an early form of *elf*.

Hawthorn: Associated with gateways as a guardian tree. Its blossoms herald the arrival of May, and here it is associated with faeries. In folk magic, the hawthorn is used to banish evil.

Hazel: Associated with wisdom and occult knowledge. It is also a tree of general protection.

Holly: Associated with regeneration in the presence of decline.

Myrtle: Associated with love. In ancient lore, it is sacred to faery beings, who in old folklore are said to live in myrtle trees.

Oak: Associated with oracle properties, and with protection. The oak symbolizes endurance and strength, and therefore holds the seasons of the year together.

Pine: Associated with purification and cleansing.

Rowan: Associated with good fortune. In ancient lore, it was associated with the theme of life and death, and was used in rites of passage to ensure renewal.

Sycamore: Associated with nurturing and with protection. Its seed pods were used in folk magic to ward off evil.

Walnut: Associated with oracle. In ancient lore, faery beings were said to be born in the walnut seed. In folk magic, the walnut was considered to bestow fertility to a couple that wanted children.

Willow: Associated with initiation and purification. In ancient lore, it was a gateway into the Underworld.

Yew: Associated with death, rebirth, and transformation.

Trees & Planetary Associations:

Sun: Laurel, birch, oak, ash, pine, walnut

Moon: Willow, olive, palm, rowan

Mars: Hickory, alder, holly, beech

Mercury: Hazel, myrtle

Jupiter: Pine, birch, mulberry, rowan

Venus: Myrtle, ash, apple, alder, sycamore, elder

Saturn: Elm, yew, alder, holly, beech

Stones:

Adventurine: Money, luck, and perception

Agate: Protection, healing, and wealth

Amber: Healing, luck, and protection

Amethyst: Dreaming, psychic natures, and happiness

Bloodstone: Healing, victory, courage, and strength

Carnelian: Protection, vitality, and health

Chalcedony: Peace and protection from nightmares

Chrysophase: Happiness, success, friendship, and luck

Citrine: Protection, psychic natures, and dreaming

Coral: Protection, power, and healing

Crystal Quartz: Protection, healing, and psychic natures

Diamond: Loyalty, harmony, and peace

Emerald: Love, money, and mental powers

Garnet: Healing, strength, and protection

Hematite: Grounding and divination

Jade: Healing, longevity, and wisdom

Jasper: Protection, tenacity, and protection

Jet: Protection, divination, and shielding

Lapis Lazuli: Healing, love, and protection

Moonstone: Divination, psychic natures, astral and dream control

Onyx: Protection, counter-magic, and balancing sex drive

Opal: Astral projection, luck, and power

Pearl: Love, wealth, and good fortune

Ruby: Wealth, protection, power, and vitality

Sapphire: Tranquility, defensive magic, and health

Tiger's Eye: Money, protection, courage, and energy

Topaz: Protection, healing, wealth, and love

Tourmaline: Love, friendship, business, and relationships

Turquoise: Protection, courage, money, friendship, and love

Stones & Planetary Associations:

Sun: Diamond, Topaz, amber, carnelian, citrine, tiger's eye

Moon: Moonstone, Opal, crystal quartz, chalcedony, pearl, sapphire

Mars: Bloodstone, Ruby, jasper, garnet

Venus: Emerald, green tourmaline, aquamarine, coral, jade, lapis, turquoise

Jupiter: Amethyst, chrysocolla, chrysoprase

Mercury: Chalcedony, citrine, agate, adventurine

Saturn: Black onyx, jet, black jade, hematite

ten

CRAFTING THE PATTERNS

Throughout the course of this book, we have examined the formulas and patterns that comprise modern Wicca. By now, you should have a working knowledge of these elements as well as a good understanding of the mechanism through which they operate. In essence you have been presented with the inner workings and the essential core of Wiccan ritual and theology. This will allow you to join the various aspects of Wiccan ritual, religion, and philosophy into a complete and cohesive system of your own making.

To aid you in creating your own system of Wicca, let's look at the process of assembling the various aspects and elements. The first step is to think about your perception of the Divine. It is here that you will create your images of the divine source, which should reflect the feminine and masculine polarities. If you want to align your system with a specific culture, then research the deity structure already in place. Focus on myths and legends in order to get a feel for how the ancient people viewed the role of the gods and goddesses. Look also for the lunar, solar, and stellar connections associated with a goddess or god figure. This will help you align the masculine and feminine connections. In other words, will the moon be feminine and the sun solar in your system? For further information regarding deity concepts review chapters one, two, three, and four.

Once your deity structure is in place, the next step is to outline the various worlds over which the deities exert influence. The most common realms will be a heaven world in which the deities dwell, along with an Underworld or Otherworld in which the dead abide. Consider also the inclusion of a mystical realm with such things as mythological beings, reincarnation, or magic. To complete this phase, think about adding the traditional doorways, including sacred wells, lakes, tree hollows, or mounds. For assistance in compiling this stage, review chapters one, five, and eight.

The next step is to establish connections to the mortal world, which will involve your deity structure and your concept of other dimensions. It is here you will decide how the deities are involved with the earth and how they interact. This phase also requires a view of how the other realms are connected. In other words, how do souls arrive in the material world, where do they go following the body's death, and how do they enter a nonmaterial realm? This is where the importance of linking the Otherworld or Underworld comes into play. Review chapters one and five for further information.

In Wicca, the role of Nature is vital, and in this regard the eight seasonal Sabbat festivals will need to be set in place. Ideally, this structure will include the mythos of the Goddess and God, depicting their relationship throughout the year. This mythical relationship expresses the aspects of each season that are experienced in life. At the core of the mythos is the theme of birth, life, death, and renewal. When constructing your seasonal tale, select a starting point for the season of the year, which in turn will be the beginning of the story of the Goddess and God in your system. You will find foundational material in chapters three, four, and six.

Another aspect to incorporate into your system centers on your view of spirits and guardian beings. Among the most common are the four elemental beings of earth, air, fire, and water. Important also are the beings known as watchers. They are typically associated with the directional quarters of the circle, but in some systems they are also connected to the elemental forces. Therefore, you will want to consider the assignment of each guardian and the type of connections you desire. Review chapters one, two, five, and six for further information.

Cosmology

You will find it very useful to establish a sound overview of your concept of cosmology as it relates to your tradition. The structure already presented in this chapter is helpful, but you should also think in terms of how this all relates to your rituals. In this regard, I include religious, ceremonial, and magical rites. This is the inner mechanism of your tradition, and everything will balance with, and pivot upon, whatever you establish.

In a sense, all the tales, myths, and legends are a part of the cosmology of our ancestors. They reveal to us the perceptions, dreams, visions, and concepts once held by the ancients. Their cosmological views can provide a sound foundation upon which to establish your tradition or system. Let's consider some of the fundamental rudiments.

Our ancestors no doubt looked upon the powerful force of Nature as the actions of supernatural beings. This seems evident in the assignment of gods and goddesses to thunder, volcanoes, earthquakes, and various types of storms. The fact that no one physically saw these gods and goddesses operate such forces points to the belief in a secret, hidden, or invisible realm. This later formed the foundation of mystical realms in myth and legend.

The light of the sun, moon, and stars must also have evoked mystery for our ancestors. One light produced heat, and another did not. Instead, it changed its shape each month. The tiny stars were points of light scattered across the night sky. They did not produce heat nor did they change shape. However, on occasion, they appeared to fall from the sky. This placed the sun, moon, and stars in the realm between the world of mortal kind and the invisible realm of the gods. They were part of our world and yet not of our world.

Attempts were made to draw upon the forces of the sun, moon, and stars. From such attempts arose a tradition of mystical correspondences that reflect the powers ascribed to the celestial lights. Rituals were created in an attempt to communicate with the sun, moon, and stars (or, more importantly, with whatever controlled them). One example is the etching of a large circle in the ground, which served as a ritual setting. The circle on the ground mimicked the circle in the sky (in this case, the moon). To stand within the circle was to enter directly into the mystical realm above.

The sun and moon appeared to rise from below the earth, and to later return beneath it. This gave rise to the idea of a realm below. The idea that the sun and moon vanished into the Underworld only to return again contributed to the concept of reincarnation. The entrance to the Underworld included the ocean, caves, wells, and lakes. The idea of a hidden world suggested inhabitants, and this played a role in the concept of faeries and other beings.

Communication with beings of the other worlds was intended to obtain favor and protection. This formed the basis of correspondences used in offerings, symbolism, evocations, and rituals. Ritual is, in effect, a means of communication with nonmaterial realms and beings. The beings known as the watchers are a good example.

When creating your view of the cosmos, think in terms of how you envision the role of other worlds. Try to see the world around as did your ancestors. In other words, seek to invoke a primal consciousness that is not tainted by scientific understandings. What and where are the connections between you and the worlds of existence? How will you contact and communicate with these realms and the beings within them? What do you want to attract and obtain? The answers will help you create something in keeping with the momentum of the past. They will also manifest what is most unique within you.

Ritual Structure

Most Wiccan rites are intended to connect with Nature or with the celestial. The former includes the eight Sabbats, and the latter involves the sun and moon. As the basis of ritual design timing, you will want to look at the various associations that pertain to Nature and celestial elements. For the Sabbats, sort them into the waxing and waning halves of the year.

The classic northern European configuration consists of the following:

Waxing: Winter Solstice, Imbolc, Spring Equinox, and Beltane

Waning: Summer Solstice, Lughnasadh, Fall Equinox, and Samhain

The classic southern European configuration consists of the following:

Waxing: Spring Equinox, Beltane, Summer Solstice, and Lughnasadh

Waning: Fall Equinox, Samhain, Yule, and Imbolc

Bear in mind that the waxing and waning periods pivot on the Winter and Summer Solstices in most Celtic systems. This means that they begin or end on the solstice day. This is symbolized by the Oak King and Holly King, who battle for reign over the year. As noted in previous chapters, the Oak King represents the waxing forces of Nature, and the Holly King symbolizes the waning forces. In southern European tradition, the waxing and waning periods of the year are marked by the equinoxes. The waxing period begins with the Spring Equinox, symbolized by the stag figure. The waning period begins with the Fall Equinox, represented by the wolf figure. Once you decide upon the waxing and waning configuration in your system, you can then begin to design the seasonal decoration theme for your Wheel of the Year rites.

The next phase of ritual design is to decide upon how to orient the sacred four directions and their elemental natures. Here you may wish to consider the area in which you live. You will want to take into consideration moisture, heat, landscape, and the prevailing winds. From this, you can make an association with earth, air, fire, and water as it presents itself in your region. Naturally, the directions of north, east, south, and west are not going to change with respect to region, but the elemental assignment to a direction can be changed accordingly. Finally, decide where earth, air, fire, and water fit best with the four directions around you. You can, if you wish, choose to go with the classic occult assignments:

North: Earth

East: Air

South: Fire

West: Water

Once the four directions are in place within your system, you can then turn your attention to the correspondences relating to other realms of existence. For example, you may wish to assign the realm of death and the departed to the western quarter (where the sun and moon return to the Underworld). You may choose to connect the eastern quarter with the evocation/invocation of divinity (where the sun and moon rise to appear on the earth). Heaven worlds can be assigned above with the celestial realm, and hidden realms (such as the faery realm) can be aligned below. Much of this will depend upon your cosmic view. In the end, you will need to work to achieve continuity so that there is no conflict between your correspondences and assignments. Look everything over and make sure it all matches and works well together.

Parting Words

If you decide to continue on now and create your own tradition, I hope this book has made the task ahead more manageable. There is one particular thought I want to leave with you. You have within you the ancestral knowledge and wisdom of those who came before you. This was passed to you just as surely as the physical traits you possess are part of your ancestral heritage. Bound within the energy that maintains your DNA is the living essence of your ancestral consciousness. This is what calls to you and evokes your feelings about nationality and place of origin. This is what stirs within you when you visit your ancestral homeland. If you sincerely seek inner guidance while working to create your own tradition, the essence of your system will be part of the past as well as the present, providing sound roots for future growth and survival.

In addition to your link to ancestral consciousness, you also possess another nature. This is the inner spark of the soul, which was generated from the creators of the universe. Your soul carries the memory of past lives, and it can possess strong ties to former lands, places, and people. In one form or another you have been in existence since the beginning of time, even if only as part of something greater than yourself. There is much you already know, and it resides deep within you. I call this place the "inner cauldron."

In ancient myth and legend, we find tales of seeking the lost or hidden cauldron. It contains a mystical brew that bestows enlightenment. Even just a small drop of this brew is said to make one wise beyond belief. The journey to find and retrieve the cauldron always takes the seeker to the Underworld or to a dark, secret dungeon. This is a metaphor for a personal journey deep within oneself. Here one finds that which was lost or hidden. It is the mystical brew that flavors the DNA spiral, itself a symbol of inward and outward movement. Here resides all that was ever known.

In some occult circles, it is believed that we do not ever create anything new; instead, we simple apply what we already know in various ways that appear new. In this light, the rituals, beliefs, and practices of Wicca are actually very old memories that we express in contemporary ways. If so, this is a very comforting and reassuring thought as you set about the task of crafting Wiccan traditions. So, what's in your cauldron? Please share it with others through your creation.

appendix i

CLASSIC WICCAN MYTHS

When Wiccan writings first surfaced with the published works of Gerald Gardner, the religion did not appear to have a creation myth. Several popular texts such as the Charge of the Goddess and the Legend of the Descent were copied from other traditions. Although many other myths have continued to appear in writings, the adoption of a popular creation myth never transpired as it did for the myths already mentioned.

The closest we can come to a published creation myth that is not modern appears in Charles Leland's book *Aradia; or the Gospel of the Witches*. I include the myth in this section as an older example. In addition, I include three key texts that complete the mythos. You can use them as templates or examples when considering what type of mythos you desire for your tradition.

Before we begin with Leland's myth, I should point out that the name "Lucifer" appears in the text, and we should recall that Lucifer was a Roman god who was the herald of the sun. He was identified with the planet Venus in its rising. In the book of Isaiah 14: 12–17 (King James Bible), the Judeo-Christian devil is called "Lucifer," based on a misunderstanding (and therefore a mistranslation) of the Hebrew name "Hillel Ben Shakhar," which means "son of the morning star," and refers to the Babylonian king of the Old Testament era. The Latin translation of the Hebrew turned Hillel Ben Shakhar into *lux ferre*, which means the light-bearer. Another Latin rendering is *lucis fer*, which means to carry light. It was St. Jerome who used this translation to link the Roman god Lucifer to the villain in Isaiah.

How Diana Made the Moon and Stars [*]

Diana was the first created before all creation; in her were all things; out of herself, the first darkness, she divided herself; into darkness and light she was divided. Lucifer, her brother and son, herself and her other half, was the light.

And when Diana saw that the light was so beautiful, the light which was her other half, her brother Lucifer, she yearned for it with exceeding great desire. Wishing to receive the light again into her darkness, to swallow it up in rapture, in delight, she trembled with desire. This desire was the Dawn.

But Lucifer, the light, fled from her, and would not yield to her wishes; he was the light which files into the most distant parts of heaven, the mouse which flies before the cat.

Then Diana went to the fathers of the Beginning, to the mothers, the spirits who were before the first spirit, and lamented unto them that she could not prevail with Lucifer. And they praised her for her courage. They told her that to rise she must fall; to become the chief of goddesses she must become a mortal.

And in the ages, in the course of time, when the world was made, Diana went on earth, as did Lucifer, who had fallen, and Diana taught magic and sorcery, whence came witches and faeries and goblins—all that is like man, yet not mortal.

And it came thus that Diana took the form of a cat. Her brother had a cat whom he loved beyond all creatures, and it slept every night on his bed, a cat beautiful beyond all other creatures, a faery: he did not know it.

---

[*] From Charles Leland, *Aradia: or the Gospel of the Witches*, first published in 1890

Diana prevailed with the cat to change forms with her, so she lay with her brother, and in the darkness assumed her own form, and so by Lucifer became the mother of Aradia. But when in the morning he found that he lay by his sister, and that light had been conquered by darkness, Lucifer was extremely angry; but Diana sang to him a spell, a song of power, and he was silent, the song of the night which soothes to sleep; he could say nothing. So Diana with her wiles of witchcraft so charmed him that he yielded to her love. This was the first fascination, she hummed the song, it was as the buzzing of bees (or a top spinning round), a spinning-wheel spinning life. She spun the lives of all men; all things were spun from the wheel of Diana. Lucifer turned the wheel.

Diana was not known to the witches and spirits, the faeries and elves who dwell in desert place, the goblins, as their mother; she hid herself in humility and was a mortal, but by her will she rose again above all. She had such passion for witchcraft, and became so powerful therein, that her greatness could not be hidden.

And thus it came to pass one night, at the meeting of all the sorceresses and faeries, she declared that she would darken the heavens and turn all the stars into mice.

All those who were present said, "If thou canst do such a strange thing, having risen to such power, thou shalt be our queen."

Diana went into the street; she took the bladder of an ox and a piece of witch-money, which has an edge like a knife—with such money witches cut the earth from men's foot tracks—and she cut the earth, and with it and many mice she filled the bladder, and blew into the bladder till it burst.

And there came a great marvel, for the earth which was in the bladder became the round heaven above, and for three days there was a great rain; the mice became stars or rain. And having made the heaven and the stars and the rain, Diana became Queen of the Witches; she was the cat who ruled the star-mice, the heaven, and the rain.

The Myth of the Descent of the Goddess†

Our Lady and Goddess would solve all mysteries, even the mystery of Death. And so she journeyed to the Underworld in her boat, upon the Sacred River of Descent. Then it came to pass that she entered before the first of the seven gates to the Underworld. And the guardians challenged her, demanding one of her garments for passage, for nothing may be received except that something be given in return. And at each of the gates the Goddess was required to pay the price of passage, for the guardians spoke to her: "Strip off your garments, and set aside your jewels, for nothing may you bring with you into this, our realm."

So the Goddess surrendered her jewels and her clothing to the guardians, and was bound as all living must be who seek to enter the realm of Death and the Mighty Ones. At the first gate she gave over her scepter, at the second her crown, at the third her necklace, at the fourth her ring, at the fifth her girdle, at the sixth her sandals, and at the seventh her gown. The Goddess stood naked and was presented before the Lord of Shadows, and such was her beauty that he himself knelt as she entered. He laid his crown and his sword at her feet, saying: "Blessed are your feet which have brought you down this path." Then he arose and said to the Goddess: "Stay with me, I pray, and receive my touch upon your heart."

And the Goddess replied to the Lord: "But I love you not, for why do you cause all the things that I love, and take delight in, to fade and die?"

"My Lady," replied the Lord. "It is age and fate against which you speak. I am helpless, for age causes all things to whither, but when men die at the end of their time, I give them rest, peace, and strength. For a time they dwell with the moon, and the spirits of the moon; then may they return to the realm of the living. But you are so lovely, and I ask you to return not, but abide with me here."

But she answered, "No, for I do not love you." Then the Lord said, "If you refuse to embrace me, then you must kneel to death's scourge."

---

† Ed. Note: This text is the author's version and expansion of earlier works by Doreen Valiente, which in turn were based on Charles Leland's *Aradia*.

The Goddess answered him: "If it is to be, then it is fate, and better so!" So she knelt in submission before the hand of Death, and he scourged her with so tender a hand that she cried out, "I know your pain, and the pain of love."

The Lord raised her to her feet and said, "Blessed are you, my Queen and my Lady." Then he gave to her the five kisses of initiation, saying: "Only thus may you attain to knowledge and to joy."

And he taught her all of his mysteries, and he gave her the necklace which is the circle of rebirth. And she taught him her mysteries of the sacred cup which is the cauldron of rebirth. They loved and joined in union with each other, and for a time the Goddess dwelled in the realm of the Lord of Shadows.

For there are three mysteries in the life of Man which are: Birth, Life, and Death (and love controls them all). To fulfill love, you must return again at the same time and place as those who loved before. And you must meet, recognize, remember, and love them anew. But to be reborn you must die and be made ready for a new body. And to die you must be born, but without love you may not be born among your own.

But our Goddess is inclined to favor love, and joy and happiness. She guards and cherishes her hidden children in this life and the next. In death she reveals the way to her communion, and in life she teaches them the magic of the mystery of the Circle (which is set between the worlds of men and of the gods).

The Legend of the Ascent of the Goddess‡

Now the time came in the Hidden Realm of Shadows that the Goddess would bear the child of the Lord of Shadows. And the Lords of the Four Corners came and beheld the newborn god. Then they spoke to the Goddess of the misery of the people who lived upon the world, and how they suffered in cold and in darkness. So she bid the Lords to carry her son to the world, and so the people rejoiced, for the Sun God had returned.

---

‡ Raven Grimassi, *The Witches' Craft*, Llewellyn, 2002.

And it came to pass that the Goddess longed for the Light of the World, and for her many children. So she journeyed to the world and was welcomed in great celebration.

Then the Goddess saw the splendor of the new god as he crossed the heavens, and she desired him. But each night he returned to the hidden realm and could not be see the beauty of the goddess in the night sky.

So one morning the goddess arose as the god came up from the hidden realm and she bathed nude in the sacred lake between the worlds. Then the Lords of the Four Corners appeared to the Sun God and said "Behold the sweet beauty of the Goddess of the Earth." And he looked upon her and was struck with her beauty so that he descended upon the earth in the form of a great stag.

"I have come to play beside your bath," he said, but the Goddess gazed upon the stag and said, "You are not a stag but a god!" Then he answered, "I am Cern, god of the forest. Yet as I stand upon the world I touch also the sky and I am Lupercus the Sun, who banishes the Wolf Night. But beyond all of this I am Tagni, the first born of all the Gods!"

The Goddess smiled and stepped forth from the water in all her beauty. "I am Fana, goddess of the forest, yet even as I stand before you I am Diana, goddess of the moon. But beyond all this I am Uni, first born of all goddesses!"

And Tagni took her by the hand and together they walked in the meadows and forests, telling their tales of ancient mysteries. They loved and were one, and together they ruled over the world. Yet even in love, Uni knew that the god would soon cross over to the hidden realm and Death would come to the world. Then must she descend and embrace the Dark Lord, and bear the fruit of their union.

The Charge of the Goddess§

Whenever you have need of anything, once in the month and better it be when the moon is full, then shall you assemble in some secret place

---

§ Versions of this text have circulated within the Wiccan community for more than 50 years, among them a similar one written by Doreen Valiente in the 1950s.

and adore the spirit of me, who am Queen of all witches. There shall ye assemble, ye who are fain to learn all sorcery, yet have not won its deepest secrets; to these will I teach all things that are as yet unknown. And ye shall be free from slavery; and as a sign that ye be truly free, you shall be naked in your rites; and ye shall dance, sing, feast, make music and love, all in my praise. For mine is the ecstasy of the spirit, and mine also is joy on earth; for my law is love unto all beings. Keep pure your highest ideals; strive ever toward them, let nothing stop you or turn you aside. For mine is the secret door which opens upon the Land of Youth, and mine is the cup of the wine of life, and the Cauldron of Cerridwen, which is the Holy Vessel of Immortality. I am the gracious Goddess, who gives the gift of joy unto the heart of man. Upon earth, I give the knowledge of the spirit eternal; and beyond death, I give peace, and freedom, and reunion with those who have gone before. Nor do I demand sacrifice; for behold, I am the Mother of all living, and my love is poured out upon the earth.

I am the beauty of the green earth, and the white moon among the stars, and the mystery of the waters, and the desire of the heart of man. Call unto thy soul, arise, and come unto me. For I am the soul of Nature, who gives life to the Universe. From me, all things proceed, and unto me all things must return; and before my face, beloved of gods and of men, let thine innermost divine self be enfolded in the rapture of the infinite. Let my worship be within the heart that rejoiceth; for behold, all acts of love and pleasure are my rituals. Therefore, let there be beauty and strength, power and compassion, honor and humility, mirth and reverence within you. And thou who thinketh to seek for me, know thy seeking and yearning shall avail thee not unless thou knoweth the mystery; that if that which thou seekest thou findest not within thee, thou wilt never find it without thee. For behold, I have been with thee from the beginning; and I am that which is attained at the end of desire.

appendix ii

GROUP RITUALS

The following rituals are intended as templates for designing your own rituals. They are complete in their presentation but you can easily add, remove, or alter the structure as desired. The value of these rituals as they are presented is that they are formed upon time-proven themes. These themes carry the energy of the momentum of the past. Therefore it is suggested that you try to retain the general framework as you create your own rituals in keeping with your needs and desires. These basic themes are outlined in previous chapters dealing with the Goddess and God and the seasons within the Wheel of the Year.

Samhain

Items required (in addition to standard altar items):

Human skull (replica / symbol) placed on the altar

1 red candle to symbolize the Goddess

1 black candle to symbolize the God

1 black candle for the skull

4 white candles for quarter points

Winter incense blend

Root of mandrake

1 small white candle for each person attending

Dried leaves (oak leaves or pine needles)

Personal offerings to the God

1 cauldron

1. Cast the circle in the usual manner.

2. Light the candle on the skull. High priest moves to the west quarter and stands before the coven members as he assumes the slain god posture. Coven members perform the Rite of Union gestures while facing high priest.

3. High priestess sounds altar bell thrice, saying:

   We gather now at this appointed time to acknowledge the absence of our Lord and Lady, they who have departed into the Hidden Realms. The Great Horned God withdraws deep into the sacred forest, and the wolf rules now in the wooded places. It is now the time of shadows and of decline. It is the time when spirits of the Otherworld return to the land of mortal kind. O ancient gods of our ancestors, bless this sacred gathering, that we who worship in your ways may be protected from the coming powers.

   Coven responds: *So mote it be!*

4. High priestess stands at the west quarter, facing the coven members, and recites the Myth of the Descent of the Goddess to the assembled coven.

   Our Lady and Goddess would solve all mysteries, even the mystery of death. And so she journeyed to the Underworld in her boat, upon the Sacred River of Descent. Then it came to pass that she entered before the first of the seven gates to the Underworld. And the guardian challenged her, demanding one of her garments for passage, for nothing may be received except that something be given in return. And at each of the gates the Goddess was required to pay the price of passage, for the guardians spoke to her: "Strip off your garments, and set aside your jewels, for nothing may you bring with you into this our realm."

So the Goddess surrendered her jewels and her clothing to the guardians, and was bound as all living must be who seek to enter the realm of Death and the Mighty Ones. At the first gate she gave over her scepter, at the second her crown, at the third her necklace, at the fourth her ring, at the fifth her girdle, at the sixth her sandals, and at the seventh her gown. The Goddess stood naked and was presented before the Lord of the Underworld, and such was her beauty that he himself knelt as she entered. He laid his crown and his sword at her feet, saying: "Blessed are your feet that have brought you down this path." Then he arose and said to her: "Stay with me I pray, and receive my touch upon your heart."

And the Goddess replied to him: "But I love you not, for why do you cause all the things that I love, and take delight in, to fade and die?"

"My Lady," replied the Lord. "It is age and fate against which you speak. I am helpless, for age causes all things to whither, but when men die at the end of their time, I give them rest, peace and strength. For a time they dwell with the moon, and the spirits of the moon; then may they return to the realm of the living. But you are so lovely, and I ask you to return not, but abide with me here."

But she answered: "No, for I do not love you." Then he said: "If you refuse to embrace me, then you must kneel to death's scourge." The Goddess answered him: "If it is to be, then it is fate, and better so!" So she knelt in submission before the hand of death, and he scourged her with so tender a hand that she cried out: "I know your pain, and the pain of love."

The God raised her to her feet and said: "Blessed are you, my Queen and my Lady." Then he gave to her the five kisses of initiation, saying: "Only thus may you attain to knowledge and to joy."

And he taught her all of his mysteries, and he gave her the necklace which is the circle of rebirth. And she taught him her mysteries of the sacred cup, which is the cauldron of rebirth. They loved and joined in union with each other, and for a time the Goddess dwelled in the realm of the Underworld.

For there are three mysteries in the life of man which are: Birth, life, and death (and love controls them all). To fulfill love, you must return again at the same time and place as those who loved before. And you must meet, recognize, remember, and love them anew. But to be reborn you must die and be made ready for a new body. And to die you must be born, but without love you may not be born among your own.

But our Goddess is inclined to favor love, and joy and happiness. She guards and cherishes her hidden children in this life and the next. In death she reveals the way to her communion, and in life she teaches them the magic of the mystery of the circle (which is set between the worlds of men and of the gods).

5. High priestess (at the west quarter) addresses coven members: *Our Goddess dwells now in the Realm of the Lord of the Shadows. The world grows cold and lifeless. But let us not sorrow for this harsh season, for all is as it must be. Therefore, let us draw close to the Lord of Shadows and embrace him. Let us find comfort in the knowledge of his essence. Blessed be all in the name of the God.*

   Coven members respond: *May the Lord of Shadows bless and protect us.*

6. High priest moves to the north and assumes the slain god posture.

7. High priestess moves to the north quarter and kneels. She touches high priest on the shoulders and groin with her left hand (tracing a triangle from his right shoulder, to left shoulder, then to groin, and back to right shoulder).

High priestess speaks:

O Ancient One, Lord of the Shadows,

Be present among us.

For now it is your time of power, O mighty Horned One.

Lord of our Passions and Desires,

This night we do welcome you in love and trust.

O Ancient One, protect us from all things in the season of decline.

8. High priestess lays her symbols and tools of rank at the high priest's feet, saying:

My Lord, I give my reign over to you,

for I know now the pains of love.

High priest takes up the symbols of the high priestess and kisses them, then places them down at the north quarter. High priest recites the Charge of the God:

Hear you all, the words of the God. By the fallen temple stone or in a forgotten glen, there shall you gather, all who seek to know my secret mysteries. For I am he who guards and he who reveals all of these things.

I am the Lord of earth and sky, of rocky cliffs and forests deep and darkened. I was there when the world was new, and I taught you to hunt and to gather plants for food. Look within yourselves, for I am there. I am that strength upon which you draw in times of need. I am that which conquers fear. I am the hero and the fool. I am your longing to be free, and your need to be bound.

In my love for you, I give up my life. I die but rise up again. I prepare the path upon which you journey, going always on before you. For it is in becoming as you, that you may become as me.

Hear the thunder, there am I. See the hawk and the raven soar, there am I. See the great wolf and the stag appear in the forest clearing, there am I. Close your eyes at the end of your days, and there am I, waiting by the temple stone.

9. Maiden places the high priestess' tools near the altar pentacle. She then leads the coven to assemble at the southern quarter.

10. High priestess (in goddess posture at the altar) faces the coven and addresses them:

    The wheel of the year has turned, cycle unto cycle, time unto time. Behold now the Lady of Shadows. I have journeyed to the hidden realm, there to prepare a place for you. The harshness of the season I leave behind me; kindle for yourselves a fire of love within, and I shall remember you, and return to you. For you are the keepers of the flame, and to all who kindle the sacred flame I shall never abandon. By the changing of the harsh season shall you know that I draw near you again. And I shall return then the greenness of plants and trees; then will you know that I have come.

    Coven responds: *We keep your sacred flame within us always, and we tend it also on the sacred altar of our rites.*

11. Each coven member now comes forward to the altar and receives a white candle. Members then move to the high priestess, who lights each candle from the goddess candle on the altar.

12. High priestess kneels before the high priest at the north quarter, lifts up the chalice (filled with wine) to him. High priest charges the wine and places his wand (tip down) into the wine within the chalice.

13. High priestess raises the chalice and offers wine to the coven, saying:

    Accept now the essence of the God.

14. In response each member goes to the high priest at the north quarter, bearing the lighted candle that they received from the altar.

    High priest addresses each member as they come, one by one, and stand before him:

    This is the light that you bore, from the season before. Accept now my essence.

    High priest snuffs out the member's candle, and bids the person to taste a small piece of mandrake root, which he first dips in the wine.

    Coven member responds: *Blessed be in the name of the God.* The person then tastes the root anointed with wine (mandrake is not chewed or ingested).

15. Coven members tread around the circle and back to the high priest. All coven members embrace the high priest with a hug. The coven reassembles at the south quarter.

16. The cauldron is brought to the west quarter and is filled with the dried leaves, lit, and set where it can be seen by all. All coven members then individually place their offerings in front of it. High priest then addresses the coven:

    Behold the womb of the Goddess of Night, which is pregnant with the Child of the coming year. O symbol of the Mystery by which we return, we honor your essence, and the magic that emanates from union with you.

    Coven members respond: *We join our desires to the seed of Light in the womb of the Goddess.*

17. High priestess addresses coven:
    Let us be secure in the protective power of the God. We shall not be in want, nor shall we suffer for we are in his care. Let us therefore feast and celebrate, all in his praise.

Coven responds: *Blessed be all in the God. Lord of the Shadows, protect us.*

18. Coven assembles in a circle, standing along the perimeter line of the ritual circle. Beginning with the high priestess, everyone will go around the circle and give the opposite sex a kiss and an embrace, saying "Many blessings," as they do so.

19. Celebration of wine and cakes begins to conclude the ritual.

20. Ritual circle is closed, candles are snuffed.

Yule (Winter Solstice)

Items required (in addition to usual ritual items):

Human skull (replica/symbol) placed on the altar

1 red candle to symbolize the Goddess

1 black candle to symbolize the God

1 black candle for the skull

4 white candles for quarter points

Winter incense blend

Personal offerings to the God

Anointing oil (solar blend)

1 cauldron

Evergreen wreath

Small log of oak

Small newborn god candle (yellow or gold) for the god flame

Cauldron for offerings

1 sprig of evergreen for each coven member

1. Cast the ritual circle in the appropriate manner.

2. High Priestess, at the altar, addresses the coven:
   We mark now, with this sacred gathering, the rebirth of the Sun God. It is the Great Mother who gives him birth. It is the lord of life born again. From the union of our Lord and Lady, hidden in the Realm of Shadows, we receive now the Child of Promise!

Coven responds: *O bring to us the Child of Promise!*

3. High priest stands at the east quarter in the god posture as high priestess addresses the four quarters. Coven members perform Rite of Union gestures to the god form as the quarters are addressed:

East: *We call forth now into the portal of the Eastern Power. We call to the ancient God, he who brought forth the light of day. We call upon the ancient God, he who was beloved of our ancient tribes.*

Coven responds: *We summon, stir, and call you forth!*

South: *We call forth now into the portal of the Southern Power. We call to the ancient God, he who brought forth the warmth of day. We call upon the ancient God, he who was beloved of our ancient tribes.*

Coven responds: *We summon, stir, and call you forth!*

West: *We call forth now into the portal of the Western Power. We call to the ancient God, he who brought forth the rain to cool the parched earth. We call upon the ancient God, he who was beloved of our ancient tribes.*

Coven responds: *We summon, stir, and call you forth!*

North: *We call forth now into the portal of the Northern Power. We call to the ancient God, he who marks the year with shadow and stone. We call upon the ancient God, he who was beloved of our ancient tribes.*

Coven responds: *We summon, stir, and call you forth!*

4. High priest (in god posture) is addressed by high priestess: *My Lord, we greet you, O Horned One, horned with the rays of the sun, by whose blessings and grace shall life always be born again. Behold, your people are gathered! Bless them and the days before them! These gifts do we give you …*

Coven responds: *Blessed be all in the name of the God.*

5. The cauldron is set before the high priest, with the coven signing the gesture of manifestation as the high priestess places an offering in front of it. Each member then places his or her offering while the other members maintain the ritual gesture. Once the last person has given an offering, the coven then assembles at the west quarter.

6. High priestess recites prayer at the altar:

   O most ancient provider, Lord of Light and Life,
   We pray you grow strong
   that we may pass the Winter in peace and fullness.
   Emanate your warmth and your Love
   that the cold and harshness of Winter
   not dwindle your followers.
   But instead fill them with your divine light
   O Ancient One, hear us!
   Protect us and provide for us in the harshness of these times.
   We give you adoration and place ourselves in your care.
   Blessed be all in the God!

   Coven responds: *Blessed be all.*

7. High priest now goes to each coven member, anoints them with the oil, and gives them a sprig of evergreen, saying:
   Blessed be in my care.

8. High priest and high priestess enact the Myth of the Season with four of the coven members, as the rest observe the drama play (which takes place at the northeast quarter).
   Narrator:
   Now the time came, in the hidden realm of Shadows, that
   the Goddess would bear the Child of the Great Lord of the
   Shadows. And the lords of the four corners came and beheld
   the newborn God. So it came to pass that the great lords were
   brought before the throne of the Shadowed One. And they
   spoke, saying: "Do we find you here in the realm of Shadow,

O Lord of Light?" And the Great One replied: "Yes, it is I. Now you have truly seen my two faces."

Then the Goddess spoke to the four lords, saying, "Take my son who is born of two lights, that he might bring new life to the world. For the earth has grown cold and lifeless." So the lords of the four corners departed to the world of men, bearing the new Lord of the Sun. And the people rejoiced, for the Lord had come that all upon the earth might be saved.

Ritualists now proceed with the drama play. The god candle is set inside the cauldron, which is set at the east quarter.

I. High priestess takes the posture for giving birth, with the cauldron placed between her legs. High priest kneels in front of her and produces a flame (lighted candle) in the manner of delivering a baby. The four lords players surround the high priest and high priestess, slightly obscuring the view of the coven members (so as to induce an air of mystery).

II. Once born, the God flame is taken by the lord of the east, who carries it to the east quarter. Here the lord presents the flame to the coven members, saying:

Hail, behold the newborn Sun.

Coven responds: *Hail Shining One, hail, Lord of the Sun.*

Each lord in turn (south, west, north) will perform the same act at associated quarter, with same coven response.

III. The east lord will tread the circle (from east quarter) to the north, taking the God flame from the north Lord and making one full pass around the circle again (holding up the God flame).

Upon returning to the north, the east lord will raise the flame to this quarter and then to the assembled coven. The east lord will then carry the God flame to the east and repeat the last act.

IV. The God flame is now carried to the altar and set upon it.

V. High priest addresses coven members:

Let your spirit be joyful and your heart despair not. For on this sacred day is born he whose Light shall save the world. He has come forth from the darkness and his Light has been seen in the east. He is Lord of Light and Life.

High priest gestures the horned god sign with hand, toward the God flame.

Behold the Sacred One, the Child of Promise! He who is born into the world, is slain for the world, and ever rises again!

VI. Now the sacred evergreen wreath is brought out and placed before the altar. The small oak log is set in the center of the wreath. The God flame is then set on top of it (symbolic of the Lord of Light and the Lord of Vegetation, being as one and the same).

9. High priest addresses assembled coven members (palms held above the God flame):

   Behold the God whose Life and Light dwells within each of us. He is the Horned One; Lord of the Forest, and the Hooded One; Lord of the Harvest, and the Old One; Lord of the Tribe. Let us therefore honor him.

Coven members place gifts for each other before the sacred evergreen, in recognition of the divinity within each person. The ritual is then concluded with the meal of cakes and wine. Celebration of the season may continue within the circle, or be taken to another location. Traditionally bonfires are set either on hilltops or upon the beach. Coven members may leap the fire, or simply toss items into the flames to "encourage the Light."

Imbolc

Items required (in addition to standard altar items):

Human skull (replica / symbol) placed on the altar

1 red candle to symbolize the Goddess

1 black candle to symbolize the God

1 black candle for the skull

4 white candles for quarter points

Winter incense blend

Personal offerings to the God

1 cauldron

Wolf-skin cloak (or representation)

Small fur or skin piece for charging chalice (traditionally wolf, or goat)

1 small candle for each coven member

God torch (candle for presentation)

1. Circle is cast in usual manner

2. High priest addresses coven members:

   We gather at this sacred time to give due praise and worship to the Lady of Fire and Lord of Ice. We mark now, at this appointed time, the young Sun God bound to winter's embrace, and the goddess who stands by the pool of fire and whose flames are the liberation through which the God can be freed.

   Coven responds: *Hail, Lady of Fire, hail, Lord of Ice.*

3. High priestess lights a torch from the altar and treads the circle from the west quarter, returning west again. She then holds the torch up to the coven.

   Coven members perform the Rite of Union gestures focused on the flame, as the maiden addresses the coven:

   Behold the Lord of Light, he who mastered the twelve labors of the great lords. He who causes the world to rejoice in his rising. He whose light brings salvation to the earth.

Coven responds: *Let his Wheel of the Year turn for us. Let the promise be fulfilled. Let the God be liberated.*

4. The high priest moves to the east quarter and assumes the god posture. High priestess kneels in front of him and begins the invocation to the God:

    Hear me, Lord of Light.

    Hear the call of Goddess, hear the call of woman.

    Breathe the scent of perfume, recall the soft touch of woman.

    Receive the hot breath of Goddess, embrace the passion of woman.

    Rise and swell, and release, release from winter's embrace.

    Coven responds, calling out three times: *Hear the call, breathe the flame, melt the ice.*

5. The guardian gives everyone a candle. Each member then moves to the north, pauses, and then proceeds to the south. There each person lights his or her candle and then moves to the east and places an offering to the Sun God.

    High priestess, at the altar, recites (as members are circling):

    O Ancient One,

    rayed in splendor and horned with power,

    be free and rise to embrace us,

    for without you we shall surely perish.

    It is now the appointed time and we offer you our worship.

    Warm now the sleeping seeds that lie beneath the cool earth,

    within the womb of the Great Mother.

    Comfort us and renew our strength!

    Behold this circle of your children;

    we have lit the ancient fires, and do faithfully serve you.

    We await your emanation of warmth.

6. High priestess goes to the east and gives chalice of wine to high priest, which he then charges (wrapping chalice in fur piece and

twisting it sunwise while visualizing the newly kindled sun rise as he gazes into the wine).

7. High priest addresses coven members:

   Behold the cool drink of Immortality. For herein is the essence of Life, and the giving of Life. Let your hearts now be joyful, and come unto me and drink of the Light of Rejuvenation. Receive this into your blood, and be fulfilled.

8. Coven members move to the high priest and receive the wine, one at a time.

9. High priestess recites the final address:

   Let us now give due praise and adoration unto the Lord of Light. For he is the symbol of the mystery by which we are reborn again. Let us always rejoice in his rising, for by this we are joined to the Essence of Rejuvenation, and Rebirth.

   Coven members respond: *Hail and adoration unto you, O Lord of Light.*

10. Coven performs the rite of cakes and wine. Celebration continues as desired until an end is called.

Ostara (Spring Equinox)

Items required (in addition to standard altar arrangement):

Human skull (replica/symbol) placed on the altar

1 red candle to symbolize the Goddess

1 black candle to symbolize the God

1 red candle for the skull

4 white candles for quarter points

Spring incense blend

Personal offerings to the God

1 cauldron

A vase (filled with water)

A reed

A scarf tied around the right thigh of the high priestess

A candle to represent the Goddess's returning light
Offerings for the Goddess
Walnut shell
Pouch of seeds tied around the high priest's waist
Large bag

1. Circle is cast in the usual manner

2. High priest addresses coven members:

    We mark now with this time of gathering, the beginning of the Ascent of our Lady from the hidden realm of Shadows. For this is the time of her desire for the Light and Life of the world. We mark the passing away of the shadow's hold and the hard embrace of winter's hand. We welcome the splendor of the new young God, rayed in power, Lord of the Sky.

    Maiden holds up the vase with the reed in it, and coven performs Rite of Union.

3. Maiden addresses coven members:

    Now it came to pass that the Goddess longed for the Light of the World, and for her many children. And she departed from the hidden realm of Shadow in secret, leaving the Lord of Shadows in dark solitude.

    Maiden continues as she recites the Myth of Ascent:

    Now the time came in the hidden realm of Shadows that the Goddess would bear the child of the Lord of the Shadows. And the lords of the four corners came and beheld the new-born god. They spoke to the Goddess of the misery of the people who lived upon the world above, and how they suffered in cold and in darkness. So the Goddess bid the lords to carry her son to the world, and so the people rejoiced, for the Sun God had returned.

    And it came to pass that the Goddess longed for the Light of the World, and for her many children. So she journeyed to the world and was welcomed in great celebration. Then the

Goddess saw the splendor of the new God as he crossed the heavens, and she desired him. But each night he returned to the hidden realm and could not see the beauty of the Goddess in the night sky. So one morning the Goddess arose as the God came up from the Hidden Realm and she bathed nude in the sacred lake. Then the Lords of the Four Corners appeared to the Sun God and said: "Behold the sweet beauty of the Goddess of the Earth."

And he looked upon her from the heights and was struck with her beauty so that he descended upon the earth and concealed himself as a reed near the bank of the lake. As the Goddess bathed in the lake she brushed against the reed, which was concealed among others. The Goddess immediately took hold of the reed and said: "You are not a reed, but a god!"

Then he answered: "Yes, I am the Lord of the Reeds. Yet when I touch the sky I am the bright blessed sun. But to be with thee I would remain a reed at thy bath."

The Goddess smiled and stepped forth from the water in all her beauty. "I am the Lady of the Lake. Yet when I touch the sky I am the sacred light of the moon. But to be with thee I would remain in the waters of this lake."

And the God took her by the hand and together they walked in the meadows and forests, telling their tales of ancient mysteries.

4. High priest moves to the east quarter and says:
   Where is my Lady?

5. High priestess, beginning at the north, moves to each quarter bearing a lighted candle, then (passing the north), stops at the east quarter.

6. Maiden replies to high priest:
   O Shadowed One, your Lady comes to us and we welcome her with great rejoicing. All living things do know that she is

near and the world stirs with life again. Our Lady journeys now to meet us and her essence is upon the forest, field, and glen.

7. High priestess calls out:

   Hear me, for now I draw near! Hear me, all who sleep from Winter's embrace, awaken unto rebirth, come forth now. Receive now my essence and be full with Life, and the desire for Life.

8. Maiden speaks to high priestess:

   O Great Goddess of the earth, return to us in your fair nature, lovely maiden of youth, and joy and love. Only you can break the spell of winter, and enchant the earth with your essence. Hail to the Great Goddess!

   Coven responds: *Hail, and praise goes to thee, Great Goddess.*

   High priestess unties the scarf around her thigh, drops it to the ground, and then assumes the goddess posture.

   Coven responds: *Hail to the Great Goddess. All praise be to thee!*

   Everyone then comes forward to the high priestess and welcomes the Goddess by embracing her with a hug, and then kneeling to touch her feet with their hands (first the left foot and then right).

   Once everyone has participated, the maiden kneels down and picks up the scarf, and gives it to the high priest (who then ties it to his cord of initiation, which is around his waist).

9. High priestess moves to the east quarter and assumes the goddess posture. Everyone comes forward and places an offering into the cauldron, which the maiden sets before the high priestess in the east. Prayers, requests, or blessings may be offered now. When completed, high priestess moves to the west quarter.

10. High priest takes a lighted torch and treads the circle to all points, thrice, beginning at the east. As he begins the third pass, four coven members (representing the lords of the four quar-

ters) stop him at the east quarter and present him to the high priestess, who now stands at the west quarter.

11. A lord addresses the high priest:

    Behold the beauty of the Goddess, she who is the Lady of the Lake, she who is the fair light of the moon in the dark sacred night.

12. High priest addresses high priestess:

    You are truly the beauty of all things. You are the earth, the sky and beyond.

13. A lord addresses the high priestess:

    Behold the power of the God. He who is Lord of the Reeds, he who is the bright sun of the blessed day.

14. High priestess addresses high priest:

    You are truly the power in all things. You are the earth, the sky, and beyond.

15. High priestess and high priest embrace each other, and the coven repeats three times:

    Blessed be the plow, the seed, and the furrow.

16. Coven then forms a circle and all of the opposite sex exchange an embrace and a kiss, as the high priestess and high priest repeat three times:

    Blessed be the plow, the seed, and the furrow.

17. While this is taking place, the maiden goes to the high priest and unties the pouch of seeds and scarf from around his waist. She then takes out three seeds and places them in the walnut shell, which she then spills out onto the scarf. The rest of the seeds are poured into the cauldron.

    The offerings are then all collected and placed within a bag. Coven members will later bury the seed pouch in a planting field (for increase of crops) or will hang it from a tree in the woods (for an abundant hunt). The offerings will be scattered around the area.

18. High priestess gives blessings over the seeds within the cauldron, saying:

> *Blessings upon these seeds, for without these we ourselves would perish from this world. Blessed be the seed that goes into the earth where deep secrets hide. There shall you lie with the elements, and spring forth as flowered plant, concealing secrets strange. In the ear of grain, spirits of the field shall come to cast their light upon you, and aid you in your growth. Through this we shall be touched by that same race, and the mysteries hidden within you shall we also obtain even unto the last of these seeds.*

The celebration concludes with wine and cakes, singing, feasting, etc.

Beltane

Items required (in addition to standard altar items):

Human skull (replica/symbol) placed on the altar
1 red candle to symbolize the Goddess
1 black candle to symbolize the God
1 red candle for the skull
4 white candles for quarter points
Spring incense blend
Personal offerings to the God
Crown wreath of flowers
Antler crown
1 small candle for each member
2 green candles and some twine to tie them together
Sword

1. Circle is cast in usual manner.

2. High priest addresses coven members:
   > *We gather at this joyous time of the courtship of our Lord and Lady. We rejoice in our queen, the Lady of the Green.*

*We rejoice in our king, the Lord of the Green. Join the dance
of Lord and Lady.*

Coven recites three times: *Seed to sprout, sprout to leaf, leaf to bud,
bud to flower, flower to fruit, fruit to seed.*

3. Maiden and guardian tie the green candles together with twine.
   The candles are then taken to the east quarter, and lighted.

4. At the northern quarter, the high priest calls down the Goddess
   upon the high priestess (who assumes the goddess posture), as
   the maiden addresses the coven:

   *By and by all things pass, season unto season, year unto year.
   The Beltane fire is kindled for our Lady of the Promised Return. We, her hidden children, do celebrate her tonight. Our
   Beltane fire burns for the young God who was bewitched by
   the beauty of the Goddess. And in love he bowed before her
   and would give his up place.*

   Coven members perform the Rite of Union to the high
   priestess, who stands in goddess posture.

5. High priest kneels before the high priestess and lays down his
   sword, saying:

   *My Lady, I give all my power to you, for this is so ordained.
   And with love I submit to you, and I give my reign over to
   your hands.*

6. High priestess takes up the sword and gives the Charge of the
   Goddess:

   *Whenever you have need of anything, once in the month
   when the moon is full, then shall you come together at some
   deserted place, or where there are woods, and give worship to
   she who is your Queen.*

   *Come all together inside a circle, and secrets that are as yet
   unknown shall be revealed. And your mind must be free and
   also your spirit, and as a sign that you are truly free, you
   shall be naked in your rites. And you shall rejoice, and sing,*

making music and love. For this is the essence of spirit, and a knowledge of joy.

Be true to your own beliefs, and keep to the Ways, beyond all obstacles. For ours is the key to the mysteries and the cycle of rebirth, which opens the way to the womb of enlightenment. I am the spirit of all the wise ones, and this is joy and peace and harmony.

In life does your Queen reveal the knowledge of spirit. And from death does the Queen deliver you to peace. Give offerings all to she who is our mother. For she is the beauty of the green earth, and the white moon among the stars, and the mystery that gives life, and always calls us to come together in her name. Let her worship be the ways within your heart, for all acts of love and pleasure are like rituals to the Goddess. But to all who seek her, know that your seeking and yearning will reward you not, until you realize the secret. Because, if that which you seek is not found within you, you will never find it from without. For she has been with you since you entered into the ways, and she is that which awaits at your journey's end.

7. High priestess moves to the east quarter, setting the sword before the altar as she goes and assumes the goddess posture. High priest gives address:

    Hail and adoration unto the Great Goddess! You who are the great Star Goddess, Queen of Heaven, Lady of the Earth; we welcome you, and rejoice in your presence.

    All coven members come forward and embrace the high priestess with a hug and a kiss. Coven then assembles in the south quarter.

8. Maiden takes a chalice of wine to the high priestess at the east quarter. Guardian takes the wand to the high priest who is also at the east quarter.

High priestess lifts the chalice up to the high priest. High priest lowers the wand into the chalice, and then the high priest and high priestess exchange a kiss.

9. High priest then leads the coven around the circle to the east quarter to receive the wine (essence of the union of Goddess and God) which they all drink.

10. High priest takes the crown of flowers and places it upon the head of the high priestess. Coven responds:

    Hail the Queen of May, hail, the Lady of the Green!

11. High priestess places the antler crown on the high priest. Coven responds:

    Hail the King of May, hail, the Lord of the Green!

The maiden and guardian lead the coven around the circle in a dance (three times around). Coven members reassemble at the south quarter. The maiden brings each member to the high priestess and high priest at the east. Each person will receive a candle (token of the Life Force) which is lit from the goddess candle on the altar, as high priestess and high priest together say:

Bear now the light of my season and walk always in balance.
May the power of the forces of light be with you.

Candles may be set aside for continuation of rite.

12. The coven forms a circle along the ritual circle's perimeter line, facing inward. Each person will then go around the circle, one at a time, kissing and embracing each member of the opposite gender.

13. Ritual celebration continues with cakes and wine, and general May merriment.

Litha (Summer Solstice)

Items required (in addition to standard ritual set-up):

    Human skull (replica/symbol) placed on the altar

    1 red candle to symbolize the Goddess

    1 black candle to symbolize the God

    1 red candle for the skull

    4 white candles for quarter points

    Summer incense blend

    Personal offerings to the God

    Flowers for procession

    Symbols for the God and Goddess

    Cauldron

    Libation fluid (nectar/ambrosia)

    4 small bowls for libation (at quarters)

    Offerings (one for deities and another for Nature spirits)

    Fennel stalk (or wood staff)

    Sorghum stalk (or wood staff)

1. Cast a circle in usual manner, then open a threshold at the northeast.

2. Coven members form a line, making a corridor (at the northeast) into the circle.

3. High priest and high priestess pass through the corridor into the circle. All members toss flowers about as the couple walks into the circle.

4. All enter the circle behind them, and then the threshold is sealed by the guardian.

5. High priestess gives address (at the altar) to the coven members:
   We gather now on this sacred night of Summer's eve, and join ourselves to the powers and forces of this mystical season. On this night the kindred gather as do all the old spirits. And on this night do they dance with the Lord of the Woods and the Lady of the Flowers in the meadows and deep woods.

Coven responds: *We sing to the Lady of Flowers, we sing to the Lord of the Woods, and we sing to the Old Ones who keep the ancient memories.*

6. Symbols of the God and Goddess are placed before the cauldron, which is set at the southern quarter. High priest addresses the coven:

   Here is the Divine Couple, whose union gives life to the world.

   Coven responds: *Blessed be all in the God and Goddess.*

   Coven performs Rite of Union facing the deity symbols.

7. Coven members now come forward and place deity offerings in the cauldron, at the south quarter.

8. Appointed members then go to each of the four quarters and pour a libation of nectar into the bowls set there for libation.

9. All coven members now place Nature spirit offerings at the four quarters.

10. High priestess speaks from the altar:
    O spirits of the Elemental forces, hear me, and receive our blessings. O spirits of the earth, O powers that be, hear me and receive our blessings. Assist us on this sacred night to maintain the natural balance, which keeps vital the essence of the earth. Let there always be clear, flowing water, freshness in the air, fertility within the soil, and abundant life within the world.

11. High priestess addresses coven members:
    On this sacred night we guard against the forces of Darkness and against all distortion. We stand with the Forces of Light, protecting the harvest and the herds. On this night we return what we have drawn through the seasons from the earth. We renew our covenant with the Old Ones. And we cleanse the surrounding ether, wrapped around our community like a

mist. As it was in the time of our beginning, so is it now, so shall it be.

Coven responds: *As it was in the time of our beginning, so is it now, so shall it be.*

High priestess and high priest then direct this drama play depicting the struggle between the forces of Light and Darkness. The fennel stalk represents the powers of Light and the sorghum stalk represents the powers of Darkness. Ritual combat begins at the east quarter and continues around the circle thrice, ending at the north. At the completion, the fennel stalk is raised in victory and is then presented at each quarter. Coven responds with cheers of approval.

12. Coven then assembles in a circle to raise the Cone of Power.¶
High priestess or high priest addresses coven members as they prepare themselves:
We form this Cone of Power to be a positive force, whereby we charge you, O Sacred Ether of our world. Be free of all evil and negativity. We charge you for the good of all life within our world.

Coven is then directed to raise the Cone of Power.

13. Once formed, the high priestess, or high priest, signals the release of power, and directs the cone up into the ether of the community.

Coven chants three times: *Up, out, and round about.*

14. End ritual with celebration of cakes and wine. Close circle. Leave libation bowls out overnight for the Nature spirits.

¶ Concerning the Cone of Power: Coven members form a circle around the high priest or high priestess (whichever is directing). The coven stands, the director sits or kneels. The method may be performed with cords or blades. Coven members joins hands and move in a clockwise circle around the director, quickening in pace as it continues. The chant should be simple, using a deity name or a word of power. When the signal to release is given, the members drop to the ground and the director quickly rises up and hurls the cone upward.

Lughnasadh

Items required (other than usual ritual items):

Human skull (replica/symbol) placed on the altar

red candle to symbolize the Goddess

1 black candle to symbolize the God

1 red candle for the skull

4 white candles for quarter points

Summer incense blend

Personal offerings to the God

1 cauldron

Offerings for the harvest

1. Circle is cast in usual manner

2. High priestess addresses coven members:

    We gather now on this appointed day in anticipation of the coming harvest. Our Lady of the Fields is ripe with child, and by her side is our Lord of the Barley. We praise the Lord and Lady and give thanks for their gifts of great bounty!

    Coven responds: *Blessed be all in the names of the Lord and Lady!*

3. Coven members are directed to give offerings at the south, as high priestess addresses them:

    Let us now go forth and give offerings to the Great God and Goddess. And let us be thankful for all we have that is good in life. For the Great Ones provide for us, and we must always remember them and give due thanks and praise.

    Chanting or singing is performed during the offerings:

    May your fields be evergreen,
    And may abundance fill you to the seam,
    And may your life be all of what you dream,
    And may the days ahead be evergreen.

    May the spirits of the earth and sky,
    Raise each stock up strong, and firm, and high,
    And may abundance fill you to the seam,

And may your fields be always evergreen.
Blessed be the plow, the seed, and the furrow.

4. High priest lights cauldron, following the offerings, at the south quarter and places a token of his needs/requests in the flames. Coven members come forth, one at a time, and do the same (requests may be written on parchment or cloth, and burned in the cauldron fire).

5. High priestess speaks at the altar, as high priest pours sweet herb incense into the cauldron flames:

   I call out to you, O Lady of the Fields and Lord of the Woods,
   and pray that you receive our wishes and desires as they rise
   up to you on the smoke of our incense. We ask that you grant
   our requests and bring them to their fullness, even as you bring
   forth the fruit from the seed.

   Coven members reply:

   By the Lady and by the Lord, so be it done.

6. High priestess addresses coven from the altar.

   Know that every action brings forth another, and that these
   actions are linked together through their natures. Therefore,
   whatsoever you send forth, so shall you receive. A farmer can
   harvest for himself no more than he plants. Therefore, let us
   consider what is good in our lives, and what is full. Let us
   also consider what is fruitless and what is empty. And let us
   consider well the reasons for all of these things.

7. High priest and high priestess bless the ritual cakes and wine. High priestess kneels with chalice of wine before the high priest. High priest lowers his wand into the wine, saying:

   Herein is joined the essence of the Lady of the Field and the
   Lord of the Woods, wherein all things are renewed and made
   vital.

High priest kneels before the high priestess, holding up the ritual cakes to her. High priestess makes the Sign of Union with her hand over them, saying:

Here is the substance of the union of the Lady of the Fields and Lord of the Woods, wherein all things are established and renewed.

Coven responds:

The two united bring forth the worlds.

8. Coven members come one at a time to receive the cakes and wine. As each one drinks of the wine, the high priest or high priestess says:

   Blessings to you in the name of the Lady and the Lord.

9. Coven reassembles at the southern quarter.

10. High priest holds up the wand, high priestess holds up the chalice (or small cauldron). High priestess speaks:

    Blessed be the plow, the seed, and the furrow.

    Coven members repeat: *Blessed be the plow, the seed, and the furrow.*

11. Coven members pair off, male and female, and join hands (for odd numbers, you can rotate).

12. Females say to males: *Blessed be your strength.*
    Males say to females: *Blessed be your magic.*
    Females say to males: *Blessed be the plow.*
    Males say to females: *Blessed be the furrow.*
    Females say to males: *Blessed be the ripened grain.*
    Males say to females: *Blessed be the vessels that nurture.*

13. High priestess and high priest say in unison:

    Blessed be the plow, the seed, and the furrow.

14. Ritual concludes with song, dance, and general merriment.

Mabon (Autumn Equinox)

Items required (other than usual ritual items):

Human skull (replica/symbol) placed on the altar

1 red candle to symbolize the Goddess

1 black candle to symbolize the God

1 red candle for the skull

4 white candles for quarter points

Autumn incense blend

Personal offerings to the God

1 cauldron

Candle to represent the God flame

Wheat shaft

Small cup or bowl (receiving vessel)

Pouch of grain tied around the waist of the high priest

Loaf of bread

Red cord to tie around god candle on altar

Dried oak leaves

Bowl for leaves

1. Circle is cast in usual manner

2. High priest at the altar says:

   We gather at this sacred time to rejoice for the abundance which has come into the world. In this we call out to the Lord of the Sheaf who falls now into Shadow, and to our Lady of the Harvest. All life comes from her and all life to her returns. The time has come when all things have grown into their fullness, and are gathered by hunter and fieldsman. As it was in the time of our beginning, so is it now, so shall it be.

   Coven responds: *Hail the Lord of the Sheaf, hail the Lady of the Harvest!*

3. High priest stands to the east, then moves west, bearing the God flame candle in one hand and the ritual wand in the other. High priestess addresses him at the west (giving him a drink from the

chalice filled with the wine of farewell, which contains a shaft of wheat):

Farewell, Lord of the Sheaf, who stands in the Light and within the Darkness. The hidden God who ever remains, and ever departs to the hidden realm through the Gate of Shadows; ruler of the Heights and of the Depths. Farewell Harvest Lord. Within you is the union of mortal and immortal. You dwell within the sacred seed, the seed of ripened grain and the seed of flesh. You are hidden in the earth, and you rise up to touch the stars.

Coven performs Rite of Union to the high priest in god posture, and then says:

Blessed be all for the bounty.

4. Female coven members go to each quarter (beginning at north) and dance from quarter to quarter. When they come to the high priest, they ritually seize him by the arms. The maiden then takes his ritual wand in her hand and, with the other females, leads him back around each quarter, returning to the west.

   Then as the females surround him in a teasing manner, the maiden unties the pouch of grain from around the high priest's waist and places it in the vessel within the cauldron. Immediately after this the maiden hands him a shaft of wheat and then extinguishes the high priest's candle flame.

   The high priest then slumps to the ground assisted by the women who lower him down.

5. High priestess addresses coven members:

   The God has departed from his abode in the fields, for the season has come and his shining vitality withers in the cool winds. And death shall come to the world for the winter draws near. The Lord of Light now becomes the Lord of the Shadows.

6. A vessel is brought out and placed in the west. Everyone will come forward, one at a time, and place some oak leaves within it. Then they will taste some of the grain which is placed beside the vessel.

7. High priestess recites a portion of the mythos:

   In the earliest times, our Lord and Lady lived in the ancient forest. Now our Lady seduced the Lord and there did she receive the sacred seed from which all things spring forth.

   But our Lord knew not the secret which only the Goddess understood, for she had drawn the life from him. And the world was abundant with all manner of animal and that which grows from the earth.

   Now there came a time when all things grew to their fullness, and were to be gathered by hunter and fieldsman alike. And in that time was the God slain and drawn into the harvest.

8. High priest is brought to the north. He is fully cloaked and his hood is drawn up over his head (which is bowed down). Female attendants hold him on each side. High priestess leads the coven from the south past him twice. Coven members bow as they pass each time.

9. A chosen female will now perform the Dance of the Descent of the Goddess, as the coven chants until the dance is complete.

10. The Hooded One assumes the god posture at the west quarter. The dancer goes and stands before the Hooded One, and the sacred dialogue begins (assign speakers):

    Goddess: *I have come in search of thee, is this where I begin?*

    God: *Begin to seek me out, and I shall become as small as a seed, so you may but pass me by.*

    Coven: *Then we shall split the rind, crack the grain, and break the pod.*

    God: *But I shall hide beneath the earth, and lay so still, that you may but pass me by.*

Goddess: *Then I shall raise you up in praise, and place upon you a mantle of green.*

God: *But I shall hide within the Green, and cover myself, and you may but pass me by.*

Coven: *Then we shall tear the husk, and pull the root and thresh the chaff.*

God: *But I shall scatter, and divide, and be so many, that you may but pass me by.*

Coven: *Then we shall gather you in, and bind you whole, and make you one again.*

11. Maiden comes forward to the altar, passing first each quarter from the north, carrying the sacred loaf of bread. High priest removes hood and resumes place among the coven (no longer impersonating the God).

12. High priestess addresses coven members (holding ritual dagger, pointed at the loaf upon the altar):
    Behold the Harvest Lord.

    Coven responds: *Blessed be the Lord of the Harvest.*

    High priestess cuts the loaf into pieces, one for each coven member. Everyone then comes forward and receives a piece of the loaf. When everyone has one, the high priestess says:

    Behold the Harvest Lord, the Lord of the Sheaf. Behold the Hidden Ones within; the Stag, the Hooded One, the King. Let us take him within us, and be as One.

    Everyone eats a piece of the loaf (but leaves a small portion to be buried in the field).

13. High Priestess passes the chalice of wine, and bids all to drink, then speaks:

    Behold, you are now as one, you are of the Royal Blood. That which was at the time of beginning, is now, and always shall be.

Coven responds: *As it was in the time of our beginning, so is it now, so shall it be. Blessed be all!*

Celebration concludes with cakes and wine, music and merriment!

appendix iii

SOLITARY RITUALS

In this appendix, you will find examples of solitary rites for the Sabbats and the full moon. Solitary rites within a tradition play a key role for the person who is not a coven member, or for coven members who are alone due to traveling or some other circumstance. Solitary rites are also helpful for providing a ritual experience for the new Wiccan without the awkwardness of performing in front of other people.

The following ritual formats are somewhat different from the group rites in the previous chapter. This will help you see how different and yet related themes can work in various ways. As with the group rituals, use the following rites as a template of examples from which you can construct your own system.

In the following rituals, you will find references to certain objects that are used in the performance of a ritual. Most of them are easy to find in various types of stores if you look long enough for them. Ideally, you would make them yourself, as this creates a stronger bond with the object, which can intensify the ritual experience. The more effort you put into the things you bring to a ritual setting, the more power you will generate. Personal effort goes a long way toward the end results. This is as true in life as it is in ritual construction.

You will find that two things happen when you make your own ritual crafts. On one level, making your own decorations and ritual paraphernalia is an act of devotion to your deities. This will strengthen and enhance not only the ritual experience but also the experience of the religion itself.

On another level, making your own ritual objects imbues them with your personal power and energy. This creates intimate alignments that deepen your connection to the ritual theme, and establishes stronger inner connections to the spirits and entities associated with any given ritual.

In the following rituals, a checklist is provided prior to the ritual script. Look the lists over so that you know ahead of time what is required. This will also provide you with a list of projects you can undertake to make your ritual objects. Any well-stocked craft store should have everything you need. You can also refer to the suggested reading list in the back of this book for other books on ritual and seasonal décor.

Samhain Ritual

Items needed:
 1 skull representation
 2 black altar candles
 1 red candle for skull image
 1 small cauldron
 1 altar bell
 2 offerings plates
 2 offerings cups
 Seasonal altar decorations
 Offerings (see ritual text)
 Ritual tools (see ritual text)
 Parchment paper
 Pen
 Matches or lighter

The key alignments of this season are Otherworld connection and creative potential. Both are related to the darkness of night (not the darkness of spirit). Therefore, you will want to use a symbol that connects to both concepts. The traditional objects are the skull and the cauldron. The skull represents the spirits in the Otherworld (literally one's ancestors). It can be made of any substance with which you feel comfortable. The cauldron represents the womb of generative life. It can be made of metal (preferred) or of heat-resistant ceramic material.

On your altar, place two black candles at the opposite end from where you will be positioned. The candles should be several inches apart, and from your perspective will be to your left and right. These candles serve as the sides of the doorway in the Otherworld. In the center of your altar place the skull and secure a red candle on its top. This will represent the living connection between you and the spirits on the other side. Red symbolizes the life force of blood.

In front of the skull, place a small cauldron. Ideally, the skull should be larger than the cauldron so that the skull is visible during the rite. Close at hand to your right, place a ritual bell. The final item needed is a small plate and a cup. You will want to place some food offerings on the plate (fruit, cheese, and beans are preferred). Pour some water, wine, or mead into the cup. This is often referred to as the meal of the dead, and is an offering to appease the spirits of the Otherworld. Place these items on your altar to the left side. This should leave some work space directly in front of you on the altar.

Place some offerings for the Goddess and God on the altar. Traditionally this can be fruit, gourds, nuts, and red wine. These offerings will be given during the ritual in addition to those made to the ancestral spirits.

When you are ready to begin, light the black candles from left to right. Ring the altar bell three times, and then recite the following:

I call to the Goddess and the God to bless this ritual, and to protect all against harm on this sacred night. I call upon my guides and guardians to gather around me and to protect me from all misdeeds.

Next, ring the bell three times, light the red candle on the skull, and say:

> *In the names of the God and Goddess, I call to the spirits beyond*
> *the veil between this world and the next. Come and partake of the*
> *offerings I freely give here upon this altar. Enter in peace and leave*
> *in peace.*

At this stage, take a piece of parchment and write a request. This should be something positive that you would like to happen in the coming twelve months. The first time you perform this rite, keep the request simple and realistic. As a guide to some possible requests, please note: Do not ask for money, ask for prosperity. Do not ask for someone specific to fall in love with you, ask that someone compatible be drawn into your life. Do not ask for revenge or harm upon another, ask to be freed from the influence or power of your enemies. The powers that be see further and with much greater wisdom than we do. Therefore, give the Universe some room to work in, and understand that the future outcome requires your full participation in achieving your goals. In Wicca, there are no free rides and you have no servants. Instead, you have faithful companions and powerful allies.

Once your request is written on the parchment, speak your wish out loud: *"In the names of the God and Goddess, I request ..."* Then fold the parchment three times and place it in the cauldron. Next, light a match, set the parchment on fire, and say:

> *By the transforming power of fire, may these words become the*
> *manifestation of my desire. Spirits of the Otherworld aid me from*
> *beyond. God and Goddess, bless my request and protect all from*
> *harm in the fulfillment of my desire.*

When the parchment is consumed, gently blow the smoke with your breath directly toward the red candle. Following this, increase the force of your next exhalations until the red candle is blown out. Then ring the bell three times and say: *"Spirits, depart now in peace, and return to your realm."* Next, gently blow the smoke from the red candle out between the two black candles. Continue until there is no longer any smoke rising from either the cauldron or the red candle.

The final phase of the ritual turns now to giving offerings to the God and Goddess. Place yours hands, palms up, one on each side of the offering plate as a welcome. Before making the offering, say:

> God and Goddess, I thank you for your presence in my life, and for walking with me along my path. Please accept this offering as a token of my love.

Once the offering phase is completed you can remove the altar items, clean them, and put them away. Take all of the ashes from the cauldron, and somewhere outside in a private place, face the east (or if wind is present, turn your back to it) and blow the ashes into the air. Imagine that the wind is carrying your desire off to be made manifest.

Winter Solstice/Yule

Items needed:

- 2 green altar candles
- 3 red candles
- 1 orange votive candle
- 1 yellow candle
- 1 evergreen wreath
- 1 Yule log
- 1 small cauldron
- 1 altar bell
- 1 offering plate
- 1 offering cup
- Seasonal altar decorations
- Offerings (see ritual text)
- Ritual tools (see ritual text)
- Matches or lighter

The key alignments of this season are rebirth and renewal. Both are related to the light of the sun. Therefore you will want to use a symbol that connects to both concepts. The traditional objects are the evergreen wreath and the yule log. The wreath represents the repeating cycle of life, as well as the promise of survival, which is symbolized by the evergreen tree. The Yule log, traditionally oak or pine, represents the sun and the Sun God. This is a symbolic remnant of tree worship from ancient times when people believed that the gods dwelled in trees.

On your altar, place two green candles at the opposite end from where you will be positioned. The candles should be several inches apart, and from your perspective will be to your left and right. These candles serve as the symbols of life in the material world and the spiritual world. Secure three red candles to the Yule log, symbolizing the vitality of the Evergreen God. In the center of your altar place the wreath, with a yellow or gold candle in the middle opening. This will represent the living connection between the sun and the promise of renewal and rebirth.

In front of the wreath, place a small cauldron with an orange votive candle inside. The altar can be decorated with other traditional symbols such as holly and mistletoe. Leave room for a ritual bell placed on the right side of the altar. The final item needed is a small plate and a cup for offerings. Nuts, sweets, and wine or mead is traditional.

When you are ready to begin, light the green candles from left to right. Ring the altar bell three times, and then recite the following:

> I call to the Goddess and the God to bless this ritual on this sacred day of rebirth.

Next, ring the bell three times, light the yellow/gold candle, and say:

> In the names of the God and Goddess, I call to the spirit of the sun who is reborn this day. Come, partake of the offerings I freely give here upon this altar, and remember your promise to return life in fullness. And through this my life too will be renewed.

At this stage, use the yellow/gold candle to light the votive candle in the cauldron. Then recite:

The fire of the Year God is passed into the Child of Promise. The Child of Light is born, the Child of Promise has come. In a new light shall I walk in the days to come.

The final phase of the ritual turns now to giving offerings to the God and Goddess. Before presenting the offerings, say:

God and Goddess, I thank you for your presence in my life, and for awakening the new light of the coming seasons. Please accept this offering as a token of my love.

Place your hands, palms up, one on each side of the offering plate as a welcome. Once the offering phase is completed, you can remove the altar items (except for the votive candle), clean them, and put them away. Allow the votive candle to burn out by itself. Afterward, clean the cauldron and put it away.

Imbolc Ritual

Items needed:
  2 white altar candles
  12 white birthday-size candles
  1 evergreen wreath (or hoop)
  1 straw man doll
  1 small cauldron
  1 altar bell
  1 offering plate
  1 offering cup
  Seasonal altar decorations
  Offerings (see ritual text)
  Ritual tools (see ritual text)
  Matches or lighter

The key alignments of this season are purity and growth. Both are related to the light of the sun. The traditional objects of this season are the candle wheel and the straw man doll. The candle wheel represents the growing cycle of life, the waxing light of the sun. You can use a hoop or a wreath to serve as the wheel and secure the candles to it. The straw man doll represents the young Sun God. This is a symbolic remnant of the Harvest Lord/Green Man image, which our ancestors believed lived in the trees and plants.

On your altar, place two white candles at the opposite end from where you will be positioned. The candles should be several inches apart, and from your perspective will be to your left and right. These candles serve as the symbols of purification in the material world and the spiritual world. In the center of your altar, place the sun wheel with the twelve white birthday candles. This will represent the living connection between the sun and the waxing cycle of Nature. In front of the sun wheel place the straw man doll.

The altar can be decorated with other traditional symbols such as pinecones and acorns. Leave room for a ritual bell, which is placed on the right side of the altar. The final item needed is a small plate for offerings of pumpkin seeds, nuts, and bread. A cup of milk is also traditional.

When you are ready to begin, light the white altar candles from left to right. Ring the altar bell three times, and then recite the following:

> I call to the Goddess and the God to bless this ritual on this sacred day of purification and growth.

Next, ring the bell three times, light the sun wheel candles, and say:

> In the names of the God and Goddess, I call to the waxing spirit of the sun. Come, partake of the offerings I freely give here upon this altar. Grow in strength and purity. Through this my life, too, is purified, and I am assured of growth in the coming seasons.

Raise the straw man doll up and pass it over the sun wheel in a full circle (moving clockwise). Then return him in front of the sun wheel. The final phase of the ritual turns now to giving offerings to the God and Goddess. Before presenting the offerings, say:

God and Goddess, I thank you for your presence in my life, and for purifying the light within and without. May your blessings of growth and increase permeate the coming seasons. Please accept this offering as a token of my love.

Place your hands, palms up, one on each side of the offering plate as a welcome. Once the offering phase is completed, you can remove the altar items (except for the sun wheel and straw man doll), clean them, and put them away. Allow the sun wheel candles to burn out. When the candles have burned away, hang the straw man doll in a window that faces east. Remove him and put him away after his first meeting with the sunrise. Later when you plant your garden, you can dip the straw man doll in water and anoint the seeds by shaking the wet doll over them.

Spring Equinox/Ostara

Items needed:
  2 green altar candles
  1 small red votive candle
  1 raw egg (in shell)
  1 small cauldron
  1 altar bell
  1 offering plate
  1 offering cup
  Seasonal altar decorations
  Offerings (see ritual text)
  Ritual tools (see ritual text)
  Matches or lighter

The key alignments of this season are regeneration and renewal. Both are related to the feminine principle in Nature. The traditional symbolic objects of this season are the egg and the cauldron. The egg represents birth in the breaking-through process, also reflected in the return of the Goddess from the Underworld. The cauldron is the womb of the Goddess, from which all things are born.

On your altar, place two green candles at the opposite end from where you will be positioned. The candles should be several inches apart, and from your perspective will be to your left and right. These candles serve as the symbols of life renewed. In the center of your altar, place the cauldron with the egg inside it. This will represent the vessel of life (in the Underworld) returning through the vessel of regeneration.

In front of the cauldron, place a small red votive candle. The altar can be decorated with other traditional symbols such as flowers, hare images, seeds, and so forth. Leave room for a ritual bell, which is placed on the right side of the altar. The final item needed is a small plate and a cup for offerings. The traditional offerings are seeds, bulbs, colored ribbons, and colored eggs.

When you are ready to begin, light the green candles from left to right. Ring the altar bell three times, and then recite the following:

> I call to the Goddess and the God to bless this ritual on this sacred day, which marks the return of life to the world.

Next, ring the bell three times, light the red votive candle, and say:

> In the names of the God and Goddess, I call to the spirit of return and regeneration. Come, partake of the offerings I freely give here upon this altar. As you awaken the sleeping seeds, awaken also the seeds of my own life that are the abilities I possess to accomplish my goals.

At this stage, take the egg from the cauldron, hold it up, and recite:

> From the darkness beneath the earth, the life-giving vessel has returned. All is rebirth, all is renewal.

Set the egg on the altar where it will be safe. The final phase of the ritual turns now to giving offerings to the God and Goddess. Before presenting the offerings, say:

God and Goddess, I thank you for your presence in my life, and for the return of life for the coming seasons. Please accept this offering as a token of my love.

Place your hands, palms up, one on each side of the offering plate as a welcome. Once the offering phase is completed, you can remove the altar items (except for the egg), clean them, and put them away.

Take the egg to your garden and crack it open on the ground. If you do not have a garden, then use a pot of soil. As you pour the egg out onto the soil, say:

The land is renewed by the return of the Goddess, the vessel of life.

Leave the egg undisturbed for twenty-four hours, and then mix it in the soil. If you're using a pot of soil, bury the egg several inches deep and leave it untouched for three days.

Afterward remove the soil, but save a handful for growing a potted plant (mix this soil with some new soil).

Beltane Ritual

Items needed:
   1 red altar candle
   1 green altar candle
   1 pink votive candle
   1 mortar and pestle
   1 small cauldron
   1 altar bell
   1 offering bowl
   1 offering cup
   Seasonal altar decorations
   Offerings (see ritual text)
   Ritual tools (see ritual text)
   Matches or lighter

The key alignments of this season are fertility and union. Both are related to the joining of the male and female polarities. The traditional object of this season is the mortar and pestle. The mortar represents the womb and the pestle symbolizes the phallus. The importance of the mortar and pestle is that it is a unified symbol that requires both elements. Separated, their intended use is lost or greatly diminished.

On your altar, place the red and green candles at the opposite end from where you will be positioned. The candles should be several inches apart, and from your perspective will be to your left (green candle) and right (red candle). These candles serve as the symbols of the male and female polarities. In the center of your altar, place the mortar and pestle side by side. Set a pink votive candle in front of the mortar and pestle.

The altar can be decorated with other traditional symbols, such as flowers and colored ribbons (red and white). Leave room for a ritual bell, which is placed on the right side of the altar. The final item needed is a small bowl for an offering of porridge, custard, or pudding. A cup of May wine is also traditional (essentially a white wine, chilled, and mixed with some strawberries and a few woodruff leaves).

When you are ready to begin, light the altar candles from left to right. Ring the altar bell three times, and then recite the following:

> I call to the Goddess and the God to bless this ritual on this sacred day of fertility and unity.

Next, ring the bell three times, light the pink candle, and say:

> In the names of the God and Goddess, I call to the essence of the feminine and masculine spirit. Come, partake of the offerings I freely give here upon this altar. Unite in creation and increase. And through this my life too shall become fertile and fruitful in the coming seasons.

Place the pestle in the mortar and say:

> Male to female, phallus to womb, energy to formation. Together they create and generate the gift of life.

The final phase of the ritual turns now to giving offerings to the God and Goddess. Before presenting the offerings, say:

God and Goddess, I thank you for your presence in my life, and for the fertile and creative essence within and without. May your blessings of fertility and fruitfulness permeate the coming seasons. Please accept this offering as a token of my love.

Place your hands, palms up, one on each side of the offering plate as a welcome. Once the offering phase is completed, you can remove the altar items (except for the mortar and pestle). If you have any seeds that you want to plant, place them in the mortar for blessings. You can also place an object in the mortar that is associated with something you wish to increase or see become fruitful—for example, the key to a business, an investment statement, etc.

Summer Solstice/Litha

Items needed:

    2 green altar candles

    1 green votive candle

    1 red rose

    1 leaf mask

    1 small cauldron

    1 altar bell

    1 offering plate

    1 offering cup

    Seasonal altar decorations

    Offerings (see ritual text)

    Ritual tools (see ritual text)

    Matches or lighter

The key alignments of this season are ripeness and rapport. The traditional objects of this season are the red rose and the leaf mask. The rose represents the Goddess in the fullness and beauty of the blossom. The leaf mask symbolizes the God in one of his primal forms linked to the land and to the sun. The fresh leaf can be oak, holly, or ivy. Eyes, nose, and a mouth should be painted or cut out on the leaf.

On your altar, place two green candles at the opposite end from where you will be positioned. The candles should be several inches apart, and from your perspective will be to your left and right. These candles serve as the symbols of ripeness and fullness. In the center of your altar place the red rose and the leaf mask side by side. This will symbolize the union of the God and Goddess. Set a green votive candle in front of them.

The altar can be decorated with a variety of flowers, and the herbs known as vervain and St. John's Wort. Leave room for a ritual bell, which is placed on the right side of the altar. The final item needed is a small plate for offerings of fruit and vegetables. A cup of mead is also traditional.

When you are ready to begin, light the altar candles from left to right. Ring the altar bell three times, and then recite the following:

> I call to the Goddess and the God to bless this ritual on this sacred day of ripeness and union.

Next, ring the bell three times, light the green votive candle, and say:

> In the names of the God and Goddess, I call to the spirit of rapport that unites all polarities. Come, partake of the offerings I freely give here upon this altar. Join and become greater than the whole. And through this my life too shall be abundant in the coming season.

The final phase of the ritual turns now to giving offerings to the God and Goddess. Before presenting the offerings, say:

> God and Goddess, I thank you for your presence in my life, and for the gift of growth and increase. May your blessings permeate the coming season. Please accept this offering as a token of my love.

Place your hands, palms up, one on each side of the offering plate as a welcome. Once the offering phase is completed, you can remove the altar items (except for the rose and leaf mask), clean them, and put them away. In a private area outside, set the rose on the ground and place the leaf mask over it. Leave them undisturbed and do not retrieve them later.

Lughnasadh Ritual

Items needed:

    2 green altar candles

    1 yellow candle (birthday size)

    1 sheaf of wheat grain

    1 cutting knife

    1 corn doll

    1 loaf of whole grain bread

    1 small cauldron

    1 altar bell

    1 offering plate

    1 offering cup

    Seasonal altar decorations

    Offerings (see ritual text)

    Ritual tools (see ritual text)

    Matches or lighter

The key alignments of this season are harvest and abundance. The traditional objects of this season are the sheaf, the blade, and the corn doll. The sheaf represents the abundant harvest, the blade is the reaper, and the corn doll is the spirit of the field. This is symbolic of the Harvest Lord figure.

On your altar, place two green candles at the opposite end from where you will be positioned. The candles should be several inches apart, and from your perspective will be to your left and right. These candles serve as the symbols of abundance and gain. In the center of your altar place the sheaf, the blade, and the corn doll next to each other. In front of this, put a whole bread loaf (unsliced, whole grain wheat is good). Place a yellow candle (birthday size) in the center of the loaf.

The altar can be decorated with other traditional symbols such as seasonal berries and other fruit. Leave room for a ritual bell, which is placed on the right side of the altar. The final item needed is a small plate for offerings of oats, corn bread, or barley cakes. A cup of mead or glass of beer is also traditional.

When you are ready to begin, light the altar candles from left to right. Ring the altar bell three times, and then recite the following:

> *I call to the Goddess and the God to bless this ritual on this sacred day of harvest and gain.*

Next, ring the bell three times, light the loaf candle, and say:

> *In the names of the God and Goddess, I call to the spirit of gathering and abundance. Come, partake of the offerings I freely give here upon this altar. Grant the fruits of all labor. And through this my life too shall be abundant and gainful in the coming seasons.*

Take the blade and lay the edge on the loaf. At the same time that you cut into the bread, also blow out the candle. Remove the candle and cut the bread into three sections. Take one small piece of bread from each section, and a cup of mead/glass of wine. Set them in front of you on the altar. Then recite:

> *For there are three great mysteries: birth, life, and death.*

Eat the three small portions of the bread and drink some of the mead/wine. Next, recite the following:

> *May I grow in knowledge and wisdom, and may the mysteries reveal themselves to me.*

The final phase of the ritual turns now to giving offerings to the God and Goddess. Before presenting the offerings, say:

> *God and Goddess, I thank you for your presence in my life, and for the abundance you grant within and without. May your blessings*

of harvest and gain permeate the coming seasons. Please accept this offering as a token of my love.

Place your hands, palms up, one on each side of the offering plate as a welcome. Once the offering phase is completed, you can remove the altar items. Pour the wine out upon the soil and toss the bread up into the air and away from you. Do not retrieve them.

Autumn Equinox/Mabon

Items needed:

    2 black altar candles
    1 black votive candle
    1 small cauldron
    1 dark mirror
    1 altar bell
    1 offering plate
    1 offering cup
    Seasonal altar decorations
    Offerings (see ritual text)
    Ritual tools (see ritual text)
    Matches or lighter

The key alignments of this season are internalization and introspection. The traditional objects of this season are the cauldron and the dark mirror. The cauldron represents the entrance to the Underworld, and the dark mirror symbolizes looking inward. For a simple dark mirror you can apply black paint to the underside of a clear piece of glass.

On your altar, place two black candles at the opposite end from where you will be positioned. The candles should be several inches apart, and from your perspective will be to your left and right. These candles serve as the symbols of the Otherworld. In the center of your altar, place the cauldron and mirror. Set a black votive candle in front of them.

The altar can be decorated with other traditional symbols, such as dried leaves and gourds. Leave room for a ritual bell, which is placed on the right side of the altar. The final item needed is a small plate for offerings of cereal grains. Place a cup of dark red wine next to the plate.

When you are ready to begin, light the altar candles from left to right. Ring the altar bell three times, and then recite the following:

> I call to the Goddess and the God to bless this ritual on this sacred day of entering into the shadows.

Next, ring the bell three times, light the votive candle, and say:

> In the names of the God and Goddess, I call to the spirit of quiet shadowed places. Come, partake of the offerings I freely give here upon this altar. Grant the inner vision and the clarity of discernment. And through this may I gain enlightenment in the places of darkness.

On a piece of parchment, write a situation in your life that needs either re-thinking or greater discernment/meditation. You can also write down anything that you want to be rid of in your life, such as smoking or some other addiction. When completed, speak your intention, fold the parchment three times, and then drop it into the cauldron. Finally, place the dark mirror over the cauldron like a lid.

The final phase of the ritual turns now to giving offerings to the God and Goddess. Before presenting the offerings, say:

> God and Goddess, I thank you for your presence in my life, and for the shadows and dark periods that help me change and grow. May your blessings of peaceful withdrawal and contemplative solitude permeate the coming season. Please accept this offering as a token of my love."

Place your hands, palms up, one on each side of the offering plate as a welcome. Once the offering phase is completed, you can remove the altar items. Take the piece of parchment, soak it in water for a few minutes, and then bury it several inches deep in some soil.

A Full Moon Ritual

Items needed:

1 altar cloth (black, if possible, to represent procreation)

1 drinking vessel

1 offering plate

1 bowl of water (add 3 pinches of salt to water and stir)

3 cookies or small cakes

Incense (of your choice; jasmine or wisteria is good)

Wine (or fruit juice)

Prepare an altar with a cloth and two white altar candles. Between these candles place your deity images (Goddess on the left, God on the right) or totems that you select to represent each deity. Place a cup (or chalice) on the altar along with a knife. Place a bowl of water on the altar where it is easily reached.

Decorate your altar with seasonal flowers and other corresponding symbols of your choosing. Set a plate of sweet cookies or cakes on the altar. Pour some wine into the drinking cup and light the incense. Then anoint your forehead, solar plexus, and stomach area with the salted water (for purification). Following this, extinguish all artificial lights, and then light the altar candles. You are now ready to begin.

Stand before the altar and look up at the moon, and say:

> On this sacred night of the Lady, beneath the full moon, which she
> has placed among the stars, I give veneration. I join on this night
> with all who gather in the name of the Goddess.

Hold your palms out (facing away from you) and form a triangle by touching the index fingers and thumbs of both hands together. Enclose the moon in the triangle opening formed between your fingers, and recite:

> Hail and adoration unto you, O great Lady. Hail, Goddess of the
> Moon, and of the Night. You have been since before the beginning,
> you who caused all things to appear, giver and sustainer of life,
> adoration unto you.

Lower your hands (releasing the triangle) and dip the fingers of your left hand into the bowl of water. Then anoint your forehead and recite:

My Lady, I pray thee impart to me thy illumination.

Anoint your eyes, and recite:

And enlighten me that I may perceive more clearly, all things in which I endeavor.

Anoint your heart area, and recite:

And illuminate my soul, imparting thy essence of purity.

Anoint your stomach and genital area by brushing your fingers down from your navel past your genitals, and then present both palms upward to the moon as you recite:

I reveal my inner self to thee and ask that all be cleansed and purified within.

Place an offering of flowers to the Goddess, setting them between your ritual tools, and recite:

O great Lady, think yet even for a moment, upon this worshipper. Beneath the sun do people toil, and go about, and attend to all worldly affairs. But beneath the moon, your children dream and awaken, and draw their power. Therefore, bless me, O great Lady, and impart to me your mystic Light, in which I find my powers. Bless me, O Lady of the Moon.

Hold the chalice of wine up to the moon, and recite:

O ancient wanderer of the dark heavens, mystery of the mysteries, emanate your sacred essence upon me as I wait below at this appointed time. Enlighten my inner mind and spirit, as do you lighten the darkness of night.

Drink from the chalice and place it back on the altar.

Place the cookies/small cakes on the pentacle, and make sure there is still some wine in the chalice. Trace a crescent over the cookies/cakes and the wine with your wand, and recite:

> *Blessings upon this meal, which is as my own body, for without such sustenance, I would perish from this world. Blessings upon the grain, which as seed went into the earth where deep secrets hide, and there did dance with the elements, and spring forth as flowered plant, concealing secrets strange. When you were in the ear of grain, spirits of the field came to cast their light upon you, and aid you in your growth. Thus through you shall I be touched by that same race, and the mysteries hidden within you, I shall obtain even unto the last of these grains.*

Trace a crescent over the wine with your athame, and recite:

> *By virtue of this sacred blade, be this wine the vital essence of the Great Goddess.*

Trace a crescent over the cakes with your wand, and recite:

> *By virtue of this sacred wand, be this cake the vital substance of the Great God.*

Lift up the pentacle and the chalice, look up at the moon, and recite:

> *Through these cakes and by this wine, may the Goddess and God bless me, and give me inner strength and vision. May I come to know that within me, which is of the eternal gods. May this blessing be so, in the names of the Lord and Lady.*

Eat a portion of the meal and drink some of the wine. Leave some for libations at the close of the ritual. The wine will be poured out on the soil and the cakes tossed up to the moon.

Sit now before the altar, look up at the moon, and visualize it as the goddess appearing to you in a sphere of light. Kiss the palm of your left hand and extend it up to her. Then say:

O bright Lady, Queen of all the Wise Ones, hear my adoration. Hear my voice as I speak your praises. Receive my words as they rise heavenward, when the full moon brightly shining fills the heavens with your beauty. See me for I come before you, and reach my hand up to you. As the full moon shines upon me, give me all your blessings.

O great Goddess of the Moon, Goddess of the mysteries of the Moon, teach me secrets yet unrevealed, ancient rites of invocation, for I believe the Wiccan's creed. And when I seek for knowledge, I seek and find you above all others.

Give me power, O most secret Lady, and protect me from my enemies. When my body lies resting nightly, speak to my inner spirit, teach me all your holy mysteries. I believe your ancient promise that all who seek your holy presence will receive of your wisdom.

Behold, O ancient Goddess, I have come beneath the full moon at this appointed time. Now the full moon shines upon me. Hear me and recall your ancient promise. Let your glory shine about me. Bless me, O gracious Queen of Heaven. In your name, so be it done.

Before completing the ritual, a work of magic or spell casting may be performed. If desired, you may wish to work with the moon bowl alignment, or Old Ways alignment. When you are finished, remove all the altar items, clean and put them away. Offer libations to the earth and the moon (pour out remaining fluids, and toss whatever remains of the cookies or cakes up toward the moon). The rite of the full moon is thereby completed.

GLOSSARY

Agreement of Consciousness: An established set of concepts, teachings, and methods that are the basis of understanding. In this regard, the matter is understood within context and relationship. In a stricter sense, an agreement of consciousness refers to pre-established and accepted norms and definitions that form the basis of understanding.

Cone of Power: An energy vortex generated by ritualists within a magical or ritual circle. It is envisioned as a swirling cone of energy that forms above the ritualists. The most common means of generating a cone of power is through dancing. Other methods such as drumming, trance, and altered states of consciousness are sometimes used or incorporated.

Cosmology: The model of the Universe and the place of all things within it. Its use in this book refers to the model created by an individual or group. It is intended to connect the various aspects and elements of a tradition together, and to present a functional and cohesive model.

Crone of the Cottage: A legendary figure in folkloric and magical traditions. In her tales, the crone was taken by the faery when she was young. She lived with them for many years, and when she returned to the mortal world so much time had passed that everyone she knew had perished long ago. The crone lives alone in a cabin deep in the woods and serves as a go-between for faeries and mortal kind. Through this she makes contact possible, which can lead to mentorship by the fFaery beings.

Group Mind: The collective thoughts and energy of a group of people that join together in common cause. This forms "one mind" with many parts that all act together in harmony and agreement. The sum of the group mind is greater than that of its parts.

Ladder of Light: A series of concepts that have formed together for the purpose of connecting realms of existence and levels of consciousness. This is envisioned as a ladder made of light, which can be used to climb upward into the higher realms of spiritual vibration, or down into the lower realms of the ancestral vibration.

Memory Chain Associations: A series of connective pathways that leapfrog back to the original source. Each idea is linked to an earlier idea that reflected yet another earlier idea of the source from which it came. By tracing backward from idea to idea, we arrive at the source, which unites us with the purity of the concept.

Momentum of the Past: A living current of energy generated by the ancestral group mind, which flows from the past to the present. It is passed through bloodlines and is an occult counterpart of our genetic patterns.

Nil Consciousness: Clearing the mind of all thoughts and perceptions. When "nothingness" prevails within the mind, the consciousness of the soul and the personality is bypassed, and for a moment we are connected directly with the perfect ideal. This informs the subconscious mind, and plants the seed of enlightenment of the conscious mind.

Otherworld: The nonmaterial realm of myth and legend where hidden and mystical realms exist, along with such beings as the elven and faery. In some myths this is the realm where mortals find rest, healing, and renewal (whether living or dead).

Perfect Ideal: The original design of creation and its purpose. This exists undiluted and nondistorted. It is the mind of the Source of All Things conceiving the universe and the purpose of everything within it.

Walker in the Woods: A spirit or entity that is attached to a place of power or a sacred site associated with a grove. It serves as both a guardian and a preserver. The walker can be communed with so that information can be received.

Wheel of Rebirth: An occult concept in which the soul is drawn back into material existence. This is caused by dense energies that are attached to the soul from its previous life or lives. These are manifestations of negative feelings, fears, regrets, and trauma of various kinds. The attachment of dense energy makes nonmaterial existence impossible, and so the soul sinks back into the world of matter to be born again.

SUGGESTED READING LIST

Ritual

First Steps in Ritual, by Dolores Ashcroft-Nowicki (Aquarian Press, 1982).

Seasonal Occult Rituals, by William Gray (London: Aquarian Press, 1970).

Inner Traditions of Magic, by William Gray (New York: Samuel Weiser, 1970).

Magical Ritual Methods, by William Gray (Cheltenham: Helios Book Service, 1971).

Western Inner Workings, by William Gray (York Beach: Samuel Weiser, 1983).

Magic

Initiation into Hermetics, by Franz Bardon (Dieter Ruggebergm 1971).

The Magician: His Training and Work, by W. E. Butler (Wilshire Book Company, 1976).

Temple Magic, by William Gray (Llewellyn Publications, 1988).

Magical States of Consciousness, by Melita Denning and Osborne Phillips (Llewellyn Publications, 1985).

Creating Magical Tools, by Chic Cicero and Sandra Tabatha Cicero (Llewellyn Publications, 1999).

Mystery Traditions

Awen, the Quest of the Celtic Mysteries, by Mike Harris (Sun Chalice Books, 1999).

The Underworld Initiation, by R. J. Stewart (Aquarian Press, 1985).

Witchcraft: A Mystery Tradition, by Raven Grimassi (Llewellyn Publications, 2005).

The Mysteries of Britain: The Secret Rites and Traditions of Ancient Britain Restored, by Lewis Spence (Newcastle Publishing, 1993).

Traditional Wicca

Witchcraft Today, by Gerald Gardner (Secaucus: Citadel Press, 1973).

The Meaning of Witchcraft, by Gerald Gardner (Samuel Weiser, 1976).

Witchcraft, A Tradition Renewed, by Doreen Valiente and Evan Jones (Custer: Phoenix Publications, 1980).

The Witches Speak, by Patricia and Arnold Crowther (Samuel Weiser, 1976).

The Secrets of Ancient Witchcraft with the Witches Tarot, by Patricia and Arnold Crowther (University Books, 1974).

Witchcraft from the Inside, by Ray Buckland (Llewellyn Publications, 1995).

West Country Wicca: A Journal of the Old Religion (Phoenix, 1989).

Pagan Religion

The Myth of the Goddess: Evolution of an Image, by Anne Baring and Jules Cashford (Arkana, 1993).

The Pagan Middle Ages, by Ludo Millis (Boydell Press, 1998).

Cities of Dreams: When Women Ruled the Earth, by Stan Gooch (Inner Traditions, 1995).

The Dream Culture of the Neanderthals, by Stan Gooch (Inner Traditions, 2006).

Christianity & Paganism in the Fourth to Eighth Centuries, by Ramsay Mac-Mullen (Yale University Press, 1997).

The Golden Bough: A Study in Magic and Religion, by James Frazer (Mac-Millan Co., 1922).

Gods & Goddesses

Dictionary of Celtic Mythology, by James MacKillop (Oxford University Press, 1998).

Who's Who in Mythology, by Alexander S. Murray (Crescent Books, 1988).

The Survival of the Pagan Gods, by Jean Seznec (Princeton University Press, 1981).

Celtic Gods, Celtic Goddesses, by R. J. Stewart (Blandford, 1990).

Making Ritual Items

Wheel of the Year: Living the Magical Life, by Pauline Campanelli and Dan Campanelli (Llewellyn Publications, 1997).

Pagan Rites of Passage, by Pauline Campanelli and Dan Campanelli (Llewellyn Publications, 1998).

BIBLIOGRAPHY

Alba, De-Anna. *The Cauldron of Change: Myths, Mysteries and Magick of the Goddess*. Oak Park: Delphi Press, 1993.

Baring, Anne and Jules Cashford. *The Myth of the Goddess: Evolution of an Image*. London: Arkana Books, 1993.

Bord, Janet and Colin Bord. *The Secret Country*. London: Paladin Book, 1980.

———. *Earth Rites*. London: Granada Publishing, 1982.

Bourne, Lois. *Witch Amongst Us: The Autobiography of a Witch*. London: Robert Hale, 1995.

Butler, W. E. *Practical Magic and the Western Mystery Tradition*. Loughborough: Thoth Publications, 2002.

———. *The Magician: His Training and Work*. Hollywood: Wilshire Book Co., 1969.

Chappell, Helen. *The Waxing Moon*. New York: Links Books, 1974.

Crowley, Vivianne. *Wicca, The Old Religion in the New Age*. Wellingborough: Aquarian Press, 1989.

Crowther, Patricia and Arnold Crowther. *The Secrets of Ancient Witchcraft with the Witches Tarot*. Secaucus: University Books, 1974.

Davies, Morganna, and Aradia Lynch. *Keepers of the Flame: Interviews with Elders of Traditional Witchcraft in America*. Providence: Olympian Press, 2001.

Elworthy, Frederick. *Horns of Honour*. London: John Murray, 1900.

Farran, David. *Living With Magic: Witchcraft and Sorcery as a New Way of Living, Loving and Expanding Our Consciousness*. New York: Simon and Schuster, 1974.

Fortune, Dion. *The Esoteric Orders and Their Work*. Wellingborough: Aquarian Press, 1982.

Frazer, James. *The Golden Bough: A Study in Magic and Religion*. New York: MacMillan Co., 1922.

Gardner, Gerald. *Witchcraft Today*. Secaucus: Citadel Press, 1973.

_____. *The Meaning of Witchcraft*. New York: Samuel Weiser, 1976.

Graves, Robert. *The White Goddess*. New York: Farrar, Straus and Giroux, 1974.

Gray, William. *Seasonal Occult Rituals*. London: Aquarian Press, 1970.

_____. *Inner Traditions of Magic*. New York: Samuel Weiser, 1970.

_____. *Magical Ritual Methods*. Cheltenham: Helios Book Service, 1971.

_____. *Western Inner Workings*. York Beach: Samuel Weiser, 1983.

Grimassi, Raven. *The Wiccan Mysteries*. St. Paul: Llewellyn Publications, 1998.

_____. *The Witches' Craft*. St. Paul: Llewellyn Publications, 2002.

_____. *Witchcraft, A Mystery Tradition*. St. Paul: Llewellyn Publications, 2004.

Hartley, Christine. *The Western Mystery Tradition*. Wellingborough: Aquarian Press, 1986.

Huson, Paul. *Mastering Witchcraft*. New York: Putnam, 1970.

Kondratiev, Alexei. *The Apple Branch: A Path to Celtic Ritual.* New York: Citadel Press, 1981.

Lang, Andrew. *Myth, Ritual & Religion,* volumes 1 & 2. London: Random House, 1996.

Leek, Sybil. *The Diary of a Witch.* New York: Signet Books, 1968.

_____. *The Complete Art of Witchcraft.* New York: Signet Books, 1971.

Matthews, John and Caitlin Matthews. *Walkers Between the Worlds: The Western Mysteries from Shaman to Magus.* Rochester: Inner Traditions, 2003.

Millis, Ludo. *The Pagan Middle Ages.* Rochester: Boydell Press, 1998.

Murray, Grace A. *Ancient Rituals and Ceremonies.* London: Alston Rivers Ltd., 1929.

Paine, Lauran. *Witchcraft and the Mysteries.* London: Robert Hale & Company, 1975.

Regardie, Israel. *The Tree of Life: A Study in Magic.* New York: Samuel Weiser, 1971.

_____. *Ceremonial Magic: A Guide to the Mechanisms of Ritual.* Wellingborough: Aquarian Press, 1980.

Sagan, Carl, and Ann Druyan. *Shadows of Forgotten Ancestors.* New York: Ballantine Books, 1992.

Seznec, Jean. *The Survival of the Pagan Gods.* Princeton: Princeton University Press, 1981.

Sheba, Lady. *The Grimoire of Lady Sheba.* St. Paul: Llewellyn Publications, 1974.

Stewart, R. J. *The Living World of Faery.* Lake Toxaway: Mercury Publishing, 1999.

Valiente, Doreen. *Witchcraft for Tomorrow.* New York: St. Martins Press, 1978.

Valiente, Doreen, and Evan Jones. *Witchcraft: A Tradition Renewed*. Custer: Phoenix Publications, 1980.

Wind, Edgar. *Pagan Mysteries in the Renaissance*. New Haven: Yale University Press, 1958.

INDEX

To Write to the Author

If you wish to contact the author or would like more information about this book, please write to the author in care of Llewellyn Worldwide and we will forward your request. Both the author and publisher appreciate hearing from you and learning of your enjoyment of this book and how it has helped you. Llewellyn Worldwide cannot guarantee that every letter written to the author can be answered, but all will be forwarded. Please write to:

Raven Grimassi
℅ Llewellyn Worldwide
2143 Wooddale Drive, Dept. 978-0-7387-1108-9
Woodbury, Minnesota 55125-2989, U.S.A.

Please enclose a self-addressed stamped envelope for reply,
or $1.00 to cover costs. If outside U.S.A., enclose
international postal reply coupon.

Many of Llewellyn's authors have websites with additional information and resources. For more information, please visit our website at http://www.llewellyn.com